THE

WHOLESOME

OVEN

THE
WHOLESOME
OVEN

successful baking without
dairy or eggs

Book Two:
Muffins, Coffee Cakes,
& Other Quick Breads

PATRICIA LESLIE, M.S.

REGENT PRESS
OAKLAND, CA

© Patricia Leslie, M.S. 2003

Library of Congress Cataloging-in-Publication Data

Leslie, Patricia, 1948-
   The wholesome oven : successful baking without dairy or
eggs / Patricia Leslie.
      p. cm.
   Includes index.
   Contents: Bk. 1. Cookies, cookies, cookies --
   ISBN 1-58790-051-3
      1. Cookery (Natural foods) 2. Baking. 1. Title

TX741.L43 2003
641.8'15--dc21

                                              2003047122

Contents: Bk. 2. Muffins, Coffee Cakes, & Other Quick Breads
ISBN 1-58790-059-9

Book design: Roz Abraham
Wheat illustration: Patricia Leslie
Manufactured in the U.S.A.
Regent Press
6020–A Adeline Street
Oakland, CA 94608
regentpress@mindspring.com

I dedicate this book to all domesticated animals everywhere — whether they sleep in our bedrooms or in barns — and to every human who is working to better their lives. Being innately gentle and trusting, all domesticated creatures deserve love, respect, care, freedom from pain and fear, and a peaceful passing at the end of their natural span of years. What human does not share the same basic needs? Therefore, to be truly happy we must bear in mind and in heart this profound truth: that whatever we do unto others indeed comes back to us — perhaps, three times over.

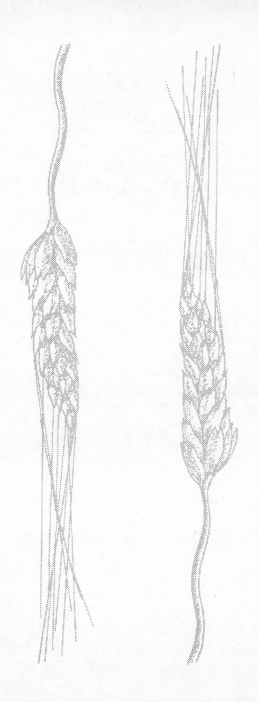

Table of Contents

One: Muffins

Some thoughts on making muffins II
Applesauce Spice Muffins I4
Apricot Muffins I6
Banana Muffins I8
Blueberry-Spelt Muffins 20
Carrot Cake Muffins 22
Cornmeal Muffins 24
Cranapple Muffins 26
Double Chocolate Muffins 28
Double Rice Muffins (Wheat-Free) 30
Four-Grain Muffins 32
Fresh Apple or Pear Muffins 34
Gingerbread Lovers' Muffins 36
Hawaiian Fantasy Muffins 38
Marmalade Muffins 40
Oat Bran Muffins 42
Simple Flavored Muffins 44

Two: Coffee Cakes, Teabreads, Toppings

Some thoughts on making coffee cakes and teabreads 47

Applesauce Ring 50

Banana Bread 52

Blueberry-Lemon Ring................................ 54

Breakfast Apple Cake 56

Carrot Coffee Cake 58

Crumb-Topped Coffee Cake 60

Date Coffee Cake 62

Fruit-Full Pear Ring 64

Fruit Preserves Coffee Cake......................... 66

Gingerbread 68

Mocha Fudge Coffee Cake (Wheat-Free) 70

Oatmeal Breakfast Cake 72

Pumpkin Spice Bread 74

Raisin Maple Loaf 76

Very Easy Teacake 78

Zucchini Bread 80

Creamy Topping 82

Crunchy Nutty Topping 83

Frozen Whipped Topping 84

Lemon Sauce 85

Vanilla Sauce... 86

Sugar Glaze 87

Three: Other Quick Breads

Some thoughts on making quick breads 89
Banana Stovetop Scones 92
Buttermilk-Style Biscuits 94
Celtic Soda Bread 96
Chocolate Scones 98
Cornbread 100
Herbed Spelt Squares 102
Lemon Scones 104
Oat Scones 106
Old-Fashioned Scones 108
Potato-Rice Biscuits (Wheat-Free) 110
Stovetop Scones 112
Surprise Scones 114
Tomato Biscuits 116

Four: Baker's Support

Useful Methods and Techniques 119
A Personal Guide to Natural Ingredients 123
Natural Product Sources 133
Company Contact Information 134
Index, by Key Flavors or Ingredients 137

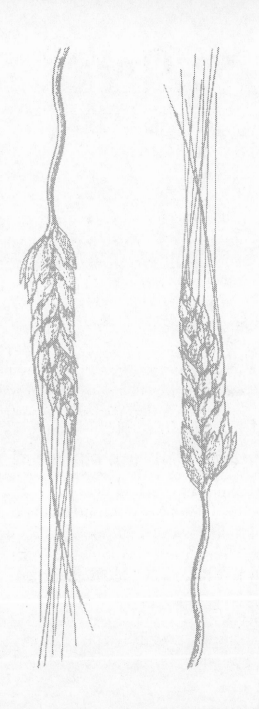

One: Muffins

SOME THOUGHTS ON MAKING MUFFINS

Muffins are a form of quick bread with a very distinctive character. Being round, self-contained, and very portable, they seem automatically qualified as a snack food. Their positive traits include being quick to whomp up, not needing to be cut into portions, and adapting themselves to an almost-infinite number of flavor and ingredient combinations. All these qualities make them ideal for lunchboxes and potlucks. But they also like to stay home, to be eaten right from the oven at breakfast, brunch, or teatime.

Like all other quick breads, muffins rely on non-yeast leavenings to do their rising. These (baking powder, baking soda, cream of tartar, or egg replacer) all react rapidly — to heat, liquid, and/or acidic ingredients. So the dough does its main rising early in the baking time, and since muffins are small, the total baking time is short.

Preparing the Muffin Pans

Muffins do better if you expose the bottoms to the air — if they sit in the pan, they "sweat" and can get a bit soggy. In my experience, nonstick pans do stick. Getting your hot muffins unstuck can be frustrating, and painful to the fingertips. So if you want to ensure that they pop out in a timely and cooperative manner, you must use oil or paper. I always used to oil my muffin pans. Now I rely on the speed and convenience of unbleached paper baking cups (page 133).

The main argument for oiling is that it is more ecologically conservative. The main drawback is that some muffins want to stick anyway. You can try sliding something down around the sides — but plastic is affected by high heat, metal will scrape off your nonstick surface quite efficiently, and most rubber spatulas aren't thin enough to do the job well. If you do use oil, the most effective is the spray-on type made with organic canola and lecithin. Spread it around with a small wad of waxed paper to get complete coverage.

In favor of baking cups, they lift right out of the pan. However, when the muffins are really hot, the paper will stick to them. When they are cool enough to eat, the paper will peel off easily. If you want to insure easy peeling, lightly spritz the paper cups with the oil spray after they are in the baking pan. The drawback is that paper is a perishable resource.

Mixing

The one thing you don't want to do is overbeat your batter after adding the flour. The more you beat, the more gluten is released from the flour, and this will result in a small, tough muffin. Beat just until the batter isn't showing any clumps of flour or extra-runny patches. Do stop and scrape the batter down from the sides of the bowl a couple of times.

If "fresh warm muffins in the morning" seems like a fine idea, I recommend that you do some preparation the night before. Measure and sift together the various dry ingredients and set them aside in a covered container. If there is dried fruit to soak, you can put it in the liquid and leave it in the fridge overnight. You can also measure and stir together liquids ahead of time and store them in the fridge. However, don't combine baking soda or egg replacer with liquid until right before baking.

Filling and Baking

The main goal is to have them come out all pretty much the same size. So I suggest filling the cups about halfway at first. Then you can judge how much batter you have left, and go around adding some to each cup.

I like to use a big soup or serving spoon to scoop up blobs of batter and plop them in. The spoon should be no wider than the tops of the cups. If you have a soft batter, try pouring it from a measuring cup. Let the dough flow out into each cup via the pour-spout. Have a small knife or spoon handy to cut off the flow.

For most muffins a bumpy, crusty, uneven top is a very appealing feature. There are a few that I prefer with a smooth, shiny top, and for those you'll find a suggestion to smooth out the tops with your fingers dipped in soymilk.

You may be used to the commercial kind of muffins that look like huge mushrooms with big "caps" domed up above the cup. These, being natural-ingredient muffins and made without eggs, don't tend to puff up like that. However, they all come out very light and tender.

APPLESAUCE SPICE MUFFINS

Makes 24

Preheat oven to 400°.
Prepare two 12-medium-cup muffin pans.

1 1/2 cups unbleached pastry flour
1/2 cup barley flour or brown rice flour
1/2 cup soymilk powder
1 teaspoon baking powder
1 teaspoon cinnamon or pumpkin pie spice

1/2 cup dates or dried pears, chopped
1/2 cup walnuts or pecans, chopped (optional)

1 cup applesauce
1/2 cup soymilk
3 tablespoons unrefined sugar
2 tablespoons canola oil
1 teaspoon apple cider vinegar
1 teaspoon baking soda

Sift together the flours, soymilk powder, baking powder and spice.
Stir in the dates or pears (and nuts) so that they are all coated with flour.

Use a mixer to beat together the applesauce, soymilk, sugar, oil, vinegar and baking soda at high speed until the mixture becomes bubbly.

Using the mixer at low speed or a fork, blend the flour mixture into the applesauce mixture, just until all the dry ingredients are fully combined. The batter can be slightly lumpy.

Use a large spoon to scoop the batter into the cups, dividing it evenly. Allow it to stay in a lumpy, "casually dropped" form — don't smooth it out.

Bake 14-15 minutes.
They will be golden brown and slightly crusty. Remove them to a rack. Serve them warm or cold.

APRICOT MUFFINS

Makes 12

Preheat oven to 375°.
Prepare a 12-medium-cup muffin pan.

1/2 cup dried apricots, cut into 1/4 inch pieces
1/2 cup juice (apple, pear, apricot or a citrus blend)

2 cups unbleached pastry flour
1/2 tablespoon baking powder

1/4 cup water
1 tablespoon egg replacer powder

1/4 cup honey or other liquid sweetener
2 tablespoons canola oil
1 teaspoon lemon peel, grated (optional)

1/3 cup cashew pieces, broken (optional)

Put the chopped apricots to soak in the juice.

Sift the flour and baking powder together.

Whisk the egg replacer powder into the water.

Add the egg replacer mixture to the sweetener, oil (and lemon peel) and beat everything together using a mixer at high speed.

Drain the apricots. Add the soaking juice to the sweetener mixture. Beat everything at high speed, just until all the ingredients are combined.
Beat the apricots in at medium speed.
Beat in the flour at medium speed just until it is fully combined.
(Fold in the cashews at low speed.)

Use a large spoon to scoop the batter into the muffin cups, dividing it evenly.

Bake 15-16 minutes.
The centers will spring back a little when pressed. They will be very pale, but the apricots (and cashews) will make little bumps on the surface, which will be browner. Remove them to a rack.
Serve them warm or cold.

BANANA MUFFINS

 Makes 16

These come out well-risen and tender. They are mildly sweet — great for breakfast! Try them spread with preserves. If you want them more dessert-like, double the sugar and do include the dates or chips.

Preheat oven to 375°.
Prepare a 12-medium-cup muffin pan, and 4 cups in a second one.

1 1/4 cups Kamut flour
1 cup brown rice flour
1 tablespoon unrefined sugar (optional)
1/2 tablespoon baking soda
1 teaspoon baking powder
1/8 teaspoon allspice (optional)

Optional:
• 3/4 cup pecans or walnuts, chopped
• 3/4 cup sliced almonds
• 1/2 cup dates, chopped
• 1/2 cup dairy-free chocolate chips

1 cup (2 or 3 average) very ripe bananas, in chunks
1 cup soy yogurt
2 tablespoons canola oil

Sift together the Kamut and rice flours, sugar, baking soda, baking powder (and allspice).
(Stir in the nuts, dates, or chocolate chips.)

In a food processor, combine the bananas, soy yogurt, and oil.
Process these ingredients together until they are fully blended.

Pour the banana mixture into the flour mixture.
Use a wooden spoon to beat everything together by hand, just until all the ingredients are fully combined.

Use a large spoon to scoop the batter into the muffin cups, dividing it evenly.

Bake 18-22 minutes.
The tops should spring back when lightly pressed. Remove them to a rack. Serve them warm or cold.

BLUEBERRY SPELT MUFFINS

 Makes 12

Preheat oven to 400°.
Prepare a 12-medium-cup muffin pan.

3/4 cup fresh or frozen blueberries
1/2 cup sliced or slivered almonds (optional)

1 1/3 cups unbleached spelt flour
1 cup quick rolled oats
1/4 cup unrefined sugar
1 tablespoon baking powder
1/2 teaspoon baking soda

1/4 cup apple or white grape juice
2 tablespoons egg replacer powder

2/3 cup soymilk
3 tablespoons canola oil
1 tablespoon honey or other liquid sweetener
2 teaspoons vanilla extract
    OR 1 teaspoon almond extract
    OR 1/2 teaspoon lemon extract

Prepare the blueberries. If they are fresh, gently wash and pat them dry. If they are frozen, thaw them, drain them, and pat them dry.

Sift together the flour, oats, sugar, baking powder and baking soda.
Stir in the blueberries (and almonds) carefully, so that they are all coated with flour.

Whisk the egg replacer powder into the juice.
Use a mixer to beat it together with the soymilk, oil, honey and flavoring at high speed until the mixture is frothy.
Using the mixer at the lowest setting, or a wooden spoon, gently fold in the flour-blueberry mixture. Stir the ingredients together just until they are fully combined.

Use a large spoon to scoop the batter into the muffin cups, filling them just up to the tops.

Bake 12-14 minutes.
These will not puff up a lot. They will be golden brown. The tops will spring back when gently pressed. Remove them to a rack. Serve them warm or cold.

CARROT CAKE MUFFINS

Makes 18

Preheat oven to 400°.
Prepare a 12-medium-cup muffin pan, and half of a second one.

1 3/4 cups barley flour
1 cup quick rolled oats (not instant)
3-6 tablespoons unrefined sugar (to taste)
1 teaspoon baking powder
1 teaspoon pumpkin pie spice
1/2 teaspoon baking soda

1/2 cup pineapple juice
1 tablespoon egg replacer powder

3/4 cup soymilk
1 tablespoon canola oil
1/2 tablespoon vanilla extract
1 teaspoon apple cider vinegar

3/4-1 cup (1 large) carrot, shredded
1/3 cup crushed pineapple, well-drained

Optional:
• 1/3 cup dates, diced
• 1/3 cup raisins
• 1/3 cup pecans, walnuts or pistachios, chopped

If you are using raisins, start them soaking in half of the pineapple juice before doing anything else.

Sift together the flour, oats, sugar, baking powder, spice and baking soda.

Whisk the egg replacer powder into the (1/4 or 1/2 cup) of pineapple juice.
Use a mixer to beat this together with the soymilk, oil, vanilla and vinegar at high speed until the mixture is frothy.
Beat in the shredded carrot and crushed pineapple at medium speed.
Beat the flour mixture into this mixture at medium speed, just until everything is fully combined.
(Use the mixer at the lowest speed, or a wooden spoon, to fold in the dates or raisins and soaking juice, and/or nuts.)
The batter will be very pourable.
Use a measuring cup to pour the batter into the muffin cups, filling them about 3/4 full.

Bake 22-24 minutes.
The tops will be golden brown. They should spring back when gently pressed. Remove them to a rack. Serve them warm or cold.

CORNMEAL MUFFINS

Makes 12

Preheat oven to 400°.
Prepare a 12-medium-cup muffin pan.

1 cup unbleached pastry flour
3/4 cup cornmeal
1/4 cup unrefined sugar
3/4 teaspoon baking soda

1/4 cup water
1 tablespoon egg replacer powder

5/8 cup soymilk
2 tablespoons canola oil
1/2 tablespoon apple cider vinegar

For tops:
1 tablespoon soymilk

Sift together the flour, cornmeal, sugar and baking soda.

Whisk the egg replacer powder into the water.
Combine it with the soymilk, oil and vinegar. Use a mixer to beat
them together at high speed until the mixture is very bubbly.
Beat in the cornmeal mixture at medium-high speed just until
all the ingredients are fully combined. The batter will be very
soft and pourable.

Use a large spoon to scoop the batter into the cups, filling them
1/2 to 3/4 full.

Use your fingers dipped in the tablespoon of soymilk to gently
smooth the tops. It is okay for them to have very small puddles
of the soymilk.

Bake 12-14 minutes.
The tops will be golden brown and crusty. They will spring
back when gently pressed. A cake tester will come out clean.
Serve them warm or cold.

CRANAPPLE MUFFINS

Makes 1 dozen

Preheat oven to 400°.
Prepare a 12-medium-cup muffin pan.

3/4 cup dried cranberries
3/8 cup apple or cranapple juice

1 1/4 cups oat bran
1/4 cup unbleached pastry flour
1/4 cup millet flour
1/2 tablespoon baking powder
1 teaspoon baking soda
1 teaspoon cinnamon

2 tablespoons apple or cranapple juice
1 tablespoon egg replacer powder

3/8 cup applesauce
1/4 cup soy yogurt (plain or vanilla)
2 tablespoons maple syrup
1/2 tablespoon canola oil
1/2 tablespoon vanilla extract

Put the dried cranberries in a small bowl with the juice to soak. Let them soak for at least 20 minutes, or as long as overnight.

Sift together the bran, pastry and millet flours, baking powder, baking soda and cinnamon.

Whisk the egg replacer powder into the 2 tablespoons of juice. Use a mixer to beat this together with the applesauce, soy yogurt, maple syrup, oil and vanilla, until the mixture is bubbly. Add the bran mixture all at once. Beat everything together at low speed, just until it turns into a mass of moist clumps. Add the cranberries and their soaking juice. Beat everything together at medium speed until they are fully combined. The batter will be very soft and a little bubbly.

Use a large spoon to scoop the batter into the muffin cups, just up to the top edges.

Bake 15-18 minutes.
A cake tester will come out clean. The tops will spring back when lightly pressed. Remove them to a rack. Serve them warm or cold.

DOUBLE CHOCOLATE MUFFINS

 Makes 12

Once these come out of the oven, it's hard to wait. But do let them cool off a bit, because the melted chips stay hot much longer than the surrounding cake.

Preheat oven to 375°.
Prepare a 12-medium-cup muffin pan.

1 1/3 cups unbleached pastry flour
1 tablespoon cocoa powder
1/2 teaspoon baking soda

1/2 cup soymilk
2 tablespoons unrefined sugar
2 tablespoons applesauce
1 tablespoon canola oil
1 teaspoon apple cider vinegar
1 teaspoon vanilla extract

3 tablespoons water
2 teaspoons egg replacer powder

3/4 cup dairy-free chocolate chips

Sift together the flour, cocoa and baking soda.

Use a mixer to beat together the soymilk, sugar, applesauce, oil, vinegar and vanilla at high speed.

Whisk the egg replacer powder into the water.
Beat this into the soymilk mixture at high speed until the mixture is frothy.
Beat in the flour mixture at low speed, just until all the ingredients are fully combined.
Fold in the chocolate chips at low speed. The batter will be very soft and pourable.

Use a measuring cup to pour the batter into the muffin cups, filling them about halfway.

Bake 14-16 minutes.
The tops will spring back when pressed. Remove them to a rack.
Serve them warm or cold.

DOUBLE RICE MUFFINS
(WHEAT-FREE)

 *Makes 12*

If rice pudding decided to be a muffin instead, it would turn into these. Try spreading them with fruit preserves. This is a tasty way to use up a small amount of leftover cooked rice.

Preheat oven to 350°.
Prepare a 12-medium-cup muffin pan.

1/4 cup raisins
2 tablespoons water

I cup brown rice flour
1/4 cup egg replacer powder
2 teaspoons baking powder
1/2 teaspoon nutmeg

5/8 cup soy yogurt
3 tablespoons canola oil
3 tablespoons maple syrup
I tablespoon apple cider vinegar
2 teaspoons vanilla extract

I cup cooked jasmine or basmati rice*

I tablespoon soymilk

Soak the raisins in the water. Set them aside to soak while you do the other steps.

Sift together the flour, egg replacer powder, baking powder and nutmeg.

Use a mixer to beat together the soy yogurt, oil, maple syrup, vinegar and vanilla at high speed until the mixture becomes a little bubbly.
Beat in the rice at medium speed until it is well combined.
Beat in the raisins and their soaking water at low speed, just until everything is fully combined.
Beat in the flour mixture at low-medium speed, just until all the ingredients are well-combined. The batter will be quite thick.

Use a big spoon to scoop the batter into the muffin cups, dividing it evenly.
Wet your fingers in the tablespoon of soymilk to smooth out the tops of the muffins.

Bake 28-30 minutes.
The tops will be very pale gold. They will not rise much, but they will spring back a little when gently pressed. Remove them to a rack. Serve them warm or cold.

* If the rice is dry and very stuck-together, mash it a bit to separate the grains before adding it to the liquids.

FOUR-GRAIN MUFFINS

Makes 18

Preheat oven to 425°.
Prepare a 12-medium-cup muffin pan and half of a second one.

1 cup unbleached pastry flour
1/2 tablespoon baking powder
3/4 teaspoon baking soda

1/2 cup blue cornmeal
1/2 cup quick oats (not instant)
1/2 cup quinoa flakes
3/8 cup unrefined sugar
1/16 teaspoon mace (optional)

1 cup soymilk
3/4 cup (1 6-ounce container) soy yogurt
1/4 cup canola oil
2 teaspoons apple cider vinegar
1/2 tablespoon vanilla

3 tablespoons water
2 tablespoons egg replacer powder

Optional:
1/2 cup dried fruit
1/2 cup chopped nuts

Sift together the flour, baking powder and baking soda.

Sift together the cornmeal, oats, quinoa flakes, sugar (and mace).

Add the soymilk, soy yogurt, oil, vinegar and vanilla. Use a mixer to beat all these ingredients together at high speed until they are fully combined.

Whisk the egg replacer powder into the water.

Add it to the cornmeal mixture. Beat it in thoroughly at medium speed.

Beat in the flour mixture at low speed, just until all the ingredients are fully combined. The batter will be very pourable.

(Fold in the dried fruit and/or nuts at low speed or by hand.)

Use a measuring cup to pour the batter into the muffin cups, dividing it evenly. Fill them to 1/4 inch below the top of the cups.

Bake 17-20 minutes.

They will be light golden brown. Remove them to a rack. Serve them warm or cold.

FRESH APPLE OR PEAR MUFFINS

 Makes 12

These are quick and simple enough to whip up for breakfast, and fantastic right out of the oven. For apples use any variety that is crisp and just a little tart. For pears, choose ripe ones with fairly firm flesh.

Preheat oven to 400°.
Prepare a 12-medium-cup muffin pan.

1 1/3 cups unbleached pastry flour
2 teaspoons baking powder
1/2 teaspoon cinnamon
   OR 1/4 teaspoon cardamom
1/4 teaspoon baking soda

1/2 cup soymilk
3 tablespoons honey or other liquid sweetener
2 tablespoons applesauce
1 tablespoon canola oil

3 tablespoons apple juice
1 tablespoon egg replacer powder

1 cup (about 1 medium) fresh apple or pear, peeled and chopped into 1/2 inch cubes

Sift together the flour, baking powder, spice and baking soda.

Whisk together the soymilk, sweetener, applesauce and oil.

Whisk the egg replacer powder into the apple juice; then whisk it into the soymilk mixture.

Stir in the apples or pears.
Use a wooden spoon to quickly stir in the flour mixture just until all the ingredients are fully combined. The batter will be quite soft and pourable.

Use a measuring cup to pour the batter into the muffin cups, dividing it evenly. Fill them about 3/4 full.

Bake 13-15 minutes.
They will be light golden. The tops will spring back when pressed. Remove them to a rack. Serve them warm or cold.

GINGERBREAD LOVERS' MUFFINS

Makes 12

These come out very soft and tender.

Preheat oven to 400°.
Prepare a 12-medium-cup muffin pan.

I I/2 cups unbleached pastry flour
2 teaspoons powdered ginger
I teaspoon pumpkin pie spice
I teaspoon baking soda

2 tablespoons white grape juice
I tablespoon egg replacer powder

3/8 cup molasses
I/4 cup applesauce
2 tablespoons canola oil

I/4 cup boiling water

Sift together the flour, ginger, pumpkin pie spice and baking soda.

Whisk the egg replacer powder into the juice.
Use a mixer to beat this together with the molasses, applesauce and oil at high speed.
Add the boiling water to this mixture and beat again at medium speed.
Add the flour mixture all at once. Beat the ingredients together quickly at medium speed. As soon as the flour disappears, stop beating. The batter will be very pourable.

Use a measuring cup to quickly pour the batter into the muffin cups, filling them about 2/3 full. Put them into the oven right away.

Bake 14-16 minutes.
The tops will spring back when gently pressed. Remove them to a rack. Serve them warm or cold.

HAWAIIAN FANTASY MUFFINS

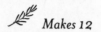 *Makes 12*

These taste just like a morning in Honolulu. So when you're yearning to drop everything and catch the next plane to the Islands, try making these. Take a bite, close your eyes, and for a few minutes you'll be transported to Waikiki.

Preheat oven to 400°.
Prepare a 12-medium-cup muffin pan.

1/2 cup pineapple juice, pineapple-coconut juice,
   or papaya nectar
1/4 cup dried pineapple, chopped in small cubes
1/4 cup dried papaya, chopped in small cubes
1/4 cup unsweetened, shredded coconut (optional)

1 1/2 cups unbleached pastry flour
2 tablespoons unrefined sugar (optional)
1/2 tablespoon baking powder
1/2 teaspoon baking soda
1/4 teaspoon powdered ginger (optional)

3/8 cup light coconut milk
2 tablespoons applesauce
1 tablespoon canola oil

3 tablespoons water
1 tablespoon egg replacer powder

1/2 cup macadamia nuts, chopped (optional)

Mix the pineapple and papaya (and coconut) into the juice. Set these aside to soak for 15-30 minutes.

Sift together the flour, (sugar), baking powder, baking soda (and ginger).

Use a mixer to beat together the coconut milk, applesauce and oil at high speed.
Whisk the egg replacer powder into the water. Add this to the coconut milk mixture, and beat everything until it is bubbly.
Fold in the fruit and its soaking juice at low speed.
Add the flour mixture and beat everything quickly at low speed, just until all the ingredients are fully combined.
(Fold in the macadamias at low speed or by hand.)

Use a large spoon to scoop the batter into the muffin cups, filling them just up to the top edges.

Bake 13-16 minutes.
They will be golden brown. The tops will spring back when gently pressed. Remove them to a rack. Serve them warm or cold.

MARMALADE MUFFINS

Makes 15–16

Preheat oven to 400°.
Prepare a 12-medium-cup muffin pan.

I 1/2 cups unbleached pastry flour
1/2 cup wheat germ
I teaspoon baking powder
1/2 teaspoon baking soda

1/2 cup lemon or orange juice
I tablespoon egg replacer powder

1/2 cup soy yogurt
1/2 cup lemon or orange marmalade*, fruit-sweetened
I tablespoon canola oil
1/2 to I tablespoon unrefined sugar (optional)
1/2 tablespoon vanilla extract
1/4 teaspoon lemon or orange extract

1/2 cup chopped pecans (optional)

Sift together the flour, wheat germ, baking powder and baking soda.

Whisk the egg replacer into the juice.
Use a mixer to beat it together with the soy yogurt, marmalade, oil, (sugar), vanilla and lemon or orange extracts at medium-high speed, until it is bubbly.
Add the flour mixture all at once and beat everything together at medium speed just until it is fully combined.
(Fold in the pecans at low speed.)
Use a large spoon to scoop the batter into the muffin cups, just up to the top edges. Put them into the oven right away.

Bake 15-17 minutes.
The tops will be golden brown. They should spring back when gently pressed. Remove them to a rack. Serve them warm or cold.

*Break up any really long strips of peel into pieces about 1/2 to 3/4 inch.

OAT BRAN MUFFINS

Makes 12

Preheat oven to 400°.
Prepare a 12-medium-cup muffin pan.

3/4 cup unbleached pastry flour
1/4 cup barley flour
1 teaspoon baking powder
1 teaspoon cinnamon
1/2 teaspoon baking soda

1/2 cup plain soy yogurt
1/2 cup soymilk
1/4 cup unrefined sugar
2 tablespoons applesauce
2 tablespoons canola oil
1 teaspoon apple cider vinegar

1 cup oat bran
1/3 cup dates, chopped, or raisins
1/3 cups nuts, chopped (optional)

3 tablespoons water
1 tablespoon egg replacer powder

Sift together the pastry and barley flours, baking powder, cinnamon and baking soda.

Use a mixer to beat together the soy yogurt, soymilk, sugar, applesauce, oil and vinegar at high speed until the mixture is very bubbly.
Beat in the bran at high speed.
Beat in the dates or raisins (and nuts) at medium speed.

Whisk the egg replacer into the water.
Beat this into the yogurt-bran mixture at medium speed.
Add the flour mixture all at once, and beat it in quickly at low to medium speed, just until all the ingredients are fully combined.

Use a large spoon to scoop the batter into the muffin cups, dividing it evenly.

Bake 17-20 minutes.
They will be well-risen and golden brown. Remove them to a rack. Serve them warm or cold.

SIMPLE FLAVORED MUFFINS

 Makes 12

These don't freeze well (an exception among the muffins in this book). But it's not likely they'll be around long enough to need freezing anyway, since they're pretty irresistible warm, split open, and spread with preserves.

Preheat oven to 375°.
Prepare a 12-medium-cup muffin pan.

1 1/2 cups unbleached pastry flour
3 tablespoons unrefined sugar
2 teaspoons baking powder

3 tablespoons canola oil

3/4 cup soymilk
1 1/2 tablespoons egg replacer powder
2 teaspoons vanilla extract
    OR 1 teaspoon lemon, orange, almond,
        or hazelnut extract

1/2 tablespoon soymilk, for tops
1 teaspoon sugar, for tops (optional)

Sift together the flour, sugar and baking powder.

Rub the oil into the flour mixture. Start with a wooden spoon. When it is fairly well worked in, switch to using your fingers. The texture will be like fine sand.

Combine the soymilk and flavored extract.

Whisk the egg replacer powder into it.

Add the flour mixture all at once. Beat with a mixer at medium speed just until all the ingredients are fully combined. The batter will be fairly thick.

Put a lump of the dough into each of the muffin cups, filling them between 2/3 and 3/4 full. Dip your fingers in the soymilk to lightly press and smooth the top of each muffin. If you wish, sprinkle a pinch of sugar over each one.

Bake 14-16 minutes.

They will be golden. The tops will spring back when gently pressed. Remove them to a rack. Serve them warm or cold.

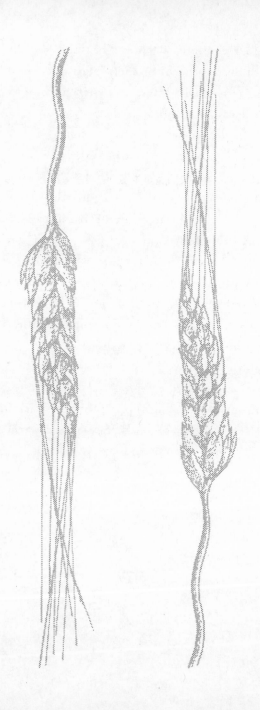

Two:
Coffee Cakes and Teabreads

SOME THOUGHTS ON MAKING COFFEE CAKES AND TEABREADS

I now realize that I have never consciously defined coffee cakes as opposed to teabreads, but I always seem to just know which is which. So I've given it some thought, and discovered there are several useful definitions. First, in my mind coffee cakes seem to be generally made in single-layer cake pans (round or square), while teabreads seem to be made in either loaf pans or ring pans. Of course this is just me. Other people seem to be comfortable with making coffee cakes in ring pans. And even a couple of my own teabreads are baked in cake pans.

So here's theory number two. This one says that coffee cakes go better with coffee, and teabreads with tea. But that also seems to be a matter of taste, since I never drink coffee, but it doesn't stop me enjoying coffee cakes.

My third and best theory is that coffee cakes are more the sort of thing to munch during a coffee break, and teabreads are for serving at afternoon (high) tea. Indeed, most of these teabreads can be spread with preserves or something creamy, or even turned into an elegant little sandwich. Many could even metamorphose into a sort of sundae, by means of fresh fruit, frozen dessert, and a sauce.

Getting Them Out of the Pan

In general, it's best to cool baked goods outside their pans. Placing them on a rack allows the air to circulate, so that they cool evenly all the way around. If they stay very hot where the cake meets the pan, while cooling at the surface, they "sweat" — moisture collects at that interface. Some are sturdy and can be removed immediately. Others have a more tender internal structure and need to cool for 10-15 minutes, to firm up before handling. A few are best left to cool completely in the pan, and for these, "sweating" doesn't seem to be a problem.

To get them out, the choices are basically oiling (or oiling/flouring) or lining. To oil, a canola-lecithin spray is best. Plain canola oil beads up, and you don't get full coverage very easily. Even with the spray, it's best to use a small wad of waxed paper to get the stuff all the way into the corners.

Flouring can help a lot with a cake that has a potential for sticking (such as a fluted-type Bundt pan). After oiling, sift a couple of tablespoons of flour all around the bottom of the pan (I use a slotted spoon). Tilt the pan back and forth, shaking and tapping it as needed to get any small clumps of flour to loosen and flow over the oiled surface. The flour will stick wherever there is oil. When all the oil has a film of flour, invert the pan over the sink and give it a couple of sharp taps to get rid of the excess flour.

It can be nerve-racking to get a cake bottom to detach completely, and parchment can make that job simple. You can line any flat-bottomed pan. Use baking parchment cut to fit the bottom, or the bottom and two sides (fold it up along the bottom corners). Of course, you will *still have to oil the uncovered areas*.

Here's how I get cakes out of pans. Two wire racks are necessary. Loosen all the edges, including the corners, and try to gently slide the knife or spatula a little way down along the bottom side, too. Gently "lever" it up and down at different spots, no more than an eighth of an inch at any one spot. See how much of the cake will lift away from the pan. If it seems to be sticking a lot, let it wait another five minutes and try this process again. When it seems like the whole bottom is loose, place a paper towel and a second wire rack over the top, grip the sides of the upper rack together with the pan (using pot holders), and quickly flip the whole thing upside-down. The cake should let go and flop the half inch or so onto the rack. Set it down. The pan will be resting upside-down on the rack, over the cake. Still using pot holders, carefully lift the pan right up and away from the cake. Now lay the first rack across the cake's bottom surface, grip both racks (the cake sandwiched between them), and flip the cake back to being right-side-up. Take the extra rack off the cake's top.

Storing

All these items should keep fine for at least two days on your kitchen counter. If the weather is cold, most will keep three days. Beyond three days, I would certainly be cautious and freeze whatever is left. These all freeze very well. Slice them before freezing. I recommend separating the slices by pieces of either waxed paper or baking parchment (cut slice-sized). You can freeze them in any handy plastic containers, or even a plastic bag. Set the slices neatly side-by-side, whatever you store them in.

APPLESAUCE RING

Makes 24–32 slices

Delicious!

Preheat oven to 325°.
Oil and flour a 10 inch Bundt or tube pan.

1 3/4 cups unbleached pastry flour
1/2 cup millet flour
1/2 cup oat bran
1/2 cup soymilk powder
1 tablespoon cinnamon
2 teaspoons baking soda

1/2 to 1 cup dates, pitted and cut into 1/2 inch pieces

1/2 cup unrefined sugar
3 tablespoons canola oil
3 tablespoons apple or white grape juice
2 tablespoons egg replacer powder
1/2 tablespoon vanilla extract
1 teaspoon fresh lemon peel, grated

3/4 cup (one 6 ounce container) soy yogurt

1 7/8 cups applesauce

Sift together the flours, bran, soymilk powder, cinnamon and baking soda. Stir the dates in so that they are all well-coated with flour.

Use a food processor, blender or mixer to beat together the sugar, oil, juice, egg replacer powder, vanilla and lemon peel until the mixture is frothy.
Add the soy yogurt and process the mixture briefly.
Add the applesauce and process the mixture just until all the ingredients are fully combined.

Beat the sugar mixture into the flour mixture, either by hand or with a mixer at medium-low speed, just until everything is combined. The batter will be very pourable.

Pour it evenly into the pan, leveling it out to the edges.

Bake 70-80 minutes.
It will be golden brown. A cake tester will come out clean. Cool it in its pan on a rack for about 20 minutes. Gently loosen it, and turn it out onto the rack to finish cooling.

BANANA BREAD

Makes 12–18 slices

Preheat oven to 350°.
Lightly oil an 8 1/2 x 4 1/2 inch loaf pan.

3/4 cup unbleached pastry flour
1/4 cup brown rice flour
1/4 cup millet flour
2 teaspoons baking powder
1/2 teaspoon baking soda
1/4 teaspoon cinnamon
1/8 teaspoon nutmeg

3/8 cup unrefined sugar
1/3 cup canola oil
1/2 tablespoon fresh orange peel, grated (optional)

1/4 cup water
2 tablespoons egg replacer powder

1 cup (about 2 average) bananas, mashed

Optional:
1/2 cup walnuts, chopped
tossed with 1 tablespoon unbleached pastry flour

Sift together the flours, baking powder, baking soda, cinnamon and nutmeg.

Use a mixer to beat together the sugar, oil (and orange peel) at high speed.

Whisk the egg replacer into the water.
Add it to the sugar mixture in two portions. Beat well at high speed each time. The mixture should become a bit bubbly.
Beat in half of the mashed banana at high speed.
Beat in half of the flour mixture at medium speed.
Beat in the rest of the mashed banana at medium speed.
Beat in the rest of the flour mixture at medium-low speed until all the ingredients are fully combined.
(Fold in the walnuts at low speed.)

Spread the batter evenly in the pan.

Bake 60-70 minutes.
A cake tester will come out clean. Allow the bread to cool in the pan for 10 minutes. Carefully loosen it and turn it out onto a wire rack. Allow it to cool completely before slicing.

BLUEBERRY-LEMON RING

Makes 24-36 slices

This will slice quite thin, very much like a pound cake.

Preheat oven to 350°.
Oil and flour a 10 inch Bundt or tube pan.

1 cup fresh or frozen blueberries
1/4 cup unbleached pastry flour

2 cups unbleached pastry flour
3/8 cup unrefined sugar
2 teaspoons baking powder
1/2 teaspoon baking soda
1 teaspoon cinnamon
    OR 1/2 teaspoon cardamom
1/4 teaspoon nutmeg or mace

1/4 cup water
2 tablespoons egg replacer powder

1 cup soy yogurt (plain or lemon)
1/4 cup soymilk (plain or vanilla)
2 tablespoons canola oil
2 tablespoons lemon juice
2 teaspoons fresh lemon peel, grated
2 teaspoons lemon extract

Prepare the blueberries. If they are fresh, gently wash and pat them dry. If they are frozen, thaw them, drain them, and pat them dry. Toss them with the 1/4 cup of flour.

Sift together the flour, sugar, baking powder, baking soda, and spices.

Whisk the egg replacer into the water.
Use a mixer to beat it together with the soy yogurt, soymilk, oil, lemon juice, lemon peel and lemon extract at high speed until the mixture becomes bubbly.
Beat in the flour mixture at medium speed until the ingredients are fully combined.
Fold in the floured blueberries at the lowest speed, or by hand.

Spread the batter evenly in the pan, leveling it out to the sides.

Bake 48-52 minutes.
The top will be golden brown. It will spring back when gently pressed. Cool the loaf in the pan for 10-15 minutes. Then carefully loosen and remove it from the pan and finish cooling it on a rack, right side up. Allow it to cool completely before slicing.

BREAKFAST APPLE CAKE

Makes 8–16 servings

Preheat oven to 350°.
Oil and flour a 9 inch round or 8 inch square pan.

Topping:
2 tablespoons unrefined sugar
1 teaspoon canola oil
1/2 teaspoon vanilla extract
1/4 cup pecans or walnuts, chopped small
    OR 1/4 cup rolled oats

Cake:
2 cups apples, peeled and chopped in 1/2 inch cubes
1/4 cup unbleached pastry flour

1 1/2 cups unbleached pastry flour
1/2 teaspoon baking powder
1/2 teaspoon baking soda
1/2 teaspoon allspice or cardamom

1/4 cup unrefined sugar
1 tablespoon egg replacer powder

5 tablespoons apple juice
2 tablespoons canola oil
1 teaspoon vanilla extract

3/4 cup (one 6-ounce container) soy yogurt

Topping:
Rub the oil and vanilla into the 2 tablespoons of sugar thoroughly. Stir in the nuts or oats.

Cake:
Toss the apples with the 1/4 cup of flour until all the pieces are coated.

Sift together the flour, baking powder, baking soda and spice.

Mix together the egg replacer and sugar.
Combine this with the apple juice, oil and vanilla. Use a mixer to beat everything together thoroughly at high speed.
Beat in half the flour mixture at medium speed.
Beat in the soy yogurt at medium speed until it is fully combined.
Beat in the rest of the flour mixture at low speed just until all the ingredients are blended. The dough will be quite stiff.
Fold in the apples by hand.

Spread the dough in the pan, pressing it out to the sides.
Sprinkle the topping evenly over the top. Press it down very lightly into the batter surface.

Bake 28-30 minutes.
The top will spring back when gently pressed. Cool it in the pan, on a rack. Allow it to mostly cool before cutting it. Serve it warm or cold.

CARROT COFFEE CAKE

Makes 16 squares

This is not a typical dense, moist, stick-to-your-ribs carrot cake. It has more of a coffee-cake texture, and an interesting interplay of flavors.

Preheat oven to 350°.
Lightly oil an 8 inch square baking pan.

2 cups unbleached pastry flour
2 teaspoons baking powder
1 teaspoon pumpkin pie spice
1/2 teaspoon baking soda

1/4 cup water
2 tablespoons egg replacer powder

3/8 cup dark brown molasses sugar
1/4 cup applesauce
1/4 cup apple juice
2 tablespoons canola oil
2 teaspoons fresh lemon peel, grated
1 teaspoon vanilla extract
1/2 teaspoon lemon extract

1 cup raw carrot, grated

Optional:
1/2 - 1 cup pecans or walnuts, chopped
1/2 - 1 cup raisins

Sift together the flour, baking powder, spice and baking soda.

Whisk the egg replacer powder into the water.
Combine this with the brown sugar, applesauce, apple juice, oil, lemon peel, vanilla and lemon extracts. Use a mixer to beat everything at high speed until it is bubbly.

Beat in the flour mixture until all the ingredients are fully combined. The dough will be fairly stiff.
Fold in the grated carrot (and nuts and/or raisins) by hand, or with the mixer at low speed.

Spread the dough out in the baking pan, leveling it to all the edges. Since the dough is sticky, the surface will have a bumpy, "knobbly" texture.

Bake 26-29 minutes.
It will be golden brown. The top should spring back when gently pressed. Cool it in the pan for 10-15 minutes, then remove it to a rack and allow it to cool completely before cutting into squares.

CRUMB-TOPPED COFFEE CAKE

Makes 8-16 pieces

Preheat oven to 350°.
Lightly oil a 9 inch round or 8 inch square baking pan.

Crumb topping:
3 tablespoons light brown muscovado sugar
3 tablespoons unbleached pastry flour
3/8 teaspoon cinnamon
1/4 teaspoon nutmeg

1 tablespoon canola oil

1 teaspoon maple syrup

Cake:
1 1/2 cups unbleached pastry flour
1 tablespoon cornstarch
1/2 tablespoon baking powder

1/2 cup soymilk
1/4 cup applesauce

3/8 cup unrefined sugar
3 tablespoons canola oil
1 teaspoon vanilla extract

2 tablespoons water
1 tablespoon egg replacer powder

Prepare the topping:

Mix together the sugar, flour, cinnamon and nutmeg.
Blend in the oil with a fork until the mixture is like fine bread crumbs. Set it aside.

Prepare the cake:

Sift together the flour, cornstarch and baking powder.

Stir together the applesauce and soymilk.

Use a mixer to beat the sugar, oil and vanilla together at high speed.
Whisk the egg replacer into the water. Beat it into the sugar mixture at high speed until the mixture is very bubbly.
Beat in half of the applesauce mixture at medium speed.
Beat in half of the flour mixture at medium speed.
Beat in the rest of the applesauce mixture at medium speed.
Beat in the rest of the flour mixture at medium speed.

Spread about 1/3 of the batter in the pan.
Sprinkle half of the crumb topping evenly over the batter.
Spread the rest of the batter over the crumb topping.

Mix the maple syrup into the remaining crumb topping. The mixture will turn into little sticky crumbs. Sprinkle them evenly over the batter surface, and slightly press them in.

Bake 33-36 minutes.
It will spring back when gently pressed. The crumb topping will be golden brown, and feel a little crispy. Cool and cut it in the pan. Serve it warm or cold.

DATE COFFEE CAKE

Makes 12–16 pieces

This cake is delicious plain, or with a topping.

Preheat oven to 375°.
Oil an 8 inch square baking pan.

1 1/2 cups dates, pitted and quartered
1 cup boiling water

1 1/3 cups unbleached pastry flour
**   OR 1 1/4 cups Kamut flour**
1/2 cup soymilk powder
3 tablespoons unrefined sugar
1 tablespoon egg replacer powder
1 teaspoon baking soda

2 tablespoons apple or white grape juice
1 tablespoon canola oil
1 tablespoon vanilla extract

1–2 teaspoons soymilk

Put the dates in a heat-proof bowl. Pour the boiling water over the dates. Allow them to soak while you do the rest of the measuring and preparation.

Sift together the flour, soymilk powder, sugar, egg replacer powder and baking soda.

Put the dates and their water in a food processor, and use the knife blade to process them until they are mostly liquefied. Add the juice, oil and vanilla. Process these ingredients until they are fully combined.

Add the flour mixture to the date mixture in the food processor in three portions. Process each time until everything is fully combined. The batter will be thick but pourable.

Immediately pour the batter into the pan, spreading it out evenly to the edges.

Dip your fingers in the soymilk and smooth the surface of the cake all over.

Bake 24-26 minutes.
The soymilk gives it a shiny, dark golden brown color when it is fully baked. The top will spring back when lightly pressed. A cake tester will come out clean. Cool it completely in the pan on a rack before cutting into squares or rectangles.

FRUIT-FULL PEAR-DATE RING

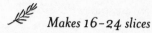 *Makes 16–24 slices*

This teabread has a wonderful flavor and texture. If you prefer apples, it will also work with them! You can serve this as a dessert — cut a thick slice for each person, lay it on its side, and pour a sauce over it.

Preheat oven to 350°.
Oil and flour a 10 inch Bundt or other tube pan.

2 cups unbleached pastry flour
2 teaspoons pumpkin pie spice
1/2 tablespoon baking soda

2 to 2 1/2 cups ripe pears, peeled, cored, cut into 1/2 inch cubes
    OR 1 (25 ounce) can or jar of pears, cubed
1 cup dates, pitted and cut in 1/2 inch pieces
1/2 cup unbleached pastry flour
1 teaspoon fresh lemon peel, grated

1/2 cup apple or pear juice
1/4 cup egg replacer powder

1/2 cup honey or other liquid sweetener
1/4 cup canola oil
1 tablespoon apple cider vinegar

Sift together the flour, spice and baking soda.

Use 2 forks to toss the dates, pastry flour and lemon peel together. Pull the pieces of date apart so that all the sides get covered. Add the pears and toss everything again. (The flour will become gluey when it touches the wet pears.)

Whisk the egg replacer powder into the juice.
Use a mixer to beat this together with the sweetener, oil and vinegar at high speed until they are very frothy.
Beat in the flour mixture at low-medium speed, just until all the ingredients are fully combined.
Fold in the fruit mixture by hand, until it is evenly distributed through the batter. It will end up as a bowl of fruit coated by batter.

Spread the batter evenly in the tube pan.

Bake 43-47 minutes.
The top will spring back when lightly pressed. The surface will be dark golden brown. Cool this in the pan on a rack for about 30 minutes. Then very carefully loosen and remove it from the pan. Allow it to finish cooling on the rack before slicing.

FRUIT PRESERVES COFFEE CAKE

Makes 8-12 pieces

Preheat oven to 350°.
Lightly oil a 9 inch round or 8 inch square pan.

1 cup unbleached pastry flour
1/4 cup unrefined sugar
1/2 teaspoon baking powder
1/2 teaspoon baking soda

1/4 cup water
1 1/2 tablespoons egg replacer powder

1/4 cup soy yogurt
1/4 cup vegan sour cream
2 tablespoons applesauce
1 tablespoon canola oil
1 teaspoon vanilla extract

4-6 tablespoons preserves, fruit-sweetened

Sift together the flour, sugar, baking powder and baking soda. Make a "well" in the middle.

Whisk the egg replacer powder into the water.

Put into the "well" the egg replacer mixture, soy yogurt, vegan sour cream, applesauce, oil and vanilla.
Use a mixer to beat everything together at medium speed for 1-2 minutes, until the mixture is well blended and a little bubbly. The batter will be thick but pourable.

Spread the batter evenly in the pan, out to the sides.
Drop blobs of the fruit preserves randomly over the top of the batter.
Use a knife or spatula to swirl the preserves over and through the upper surface of the batter. If necessary, smooth the surface out again so that it is fairly level, without any large "hills or valleys."

Bake 27-30 minutes.
The top will be golden brown. Cool it in the pan, on a rack. Serve it warm or cold.

GINGERBREAD

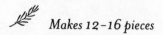 *Makes 12-16 pieces*

You can serve this cold, like a bar cookie. Or you can serve it warm, with a creamy topping or vanilla frozen dessert. It cuts best when cold, but is most tempting when warm!

Preheat oven to 350°.
Lightly oil an 8x8 inch baking pan.

1 cup unbleached pastry flour
3/4 cup spelt flour
2 teaspoons ginger
1/2 teaspoon cinnamon
1/4 teaspoon cloves

1/2 cup molasses
1/4 cup unrefined sugar
2 tablespoons canola oil

3 tablespoons apple juice
1 tablespoon egg replacer powder

1/2 cup boiling water
3/4 teaspoon baking soda

Sift together the pastry and spelt flours, ginger, cinnamon and cloves.

Use a mixer to beat together the molasses, sugar and oil at high speed, until the mixture is frothy.

Whisk the egg replacer powder into the apple juice.
Add it to the molasses mixture, and beat it in at high speed until the mixture is bubbly.
Add the flour mixture all at once to the molasses mixture. Beat these ingredients together at medium speed until they are fully combined. The batter will be quite thick and sticky.

Put the baking soda in a glass measuring cup.
Pour the boiling water in (up to the 1/2 cup measure) and stir just until the soda is dissolved.
Add this water to the batter. Beat all the ingredients together at high speed until they are fully blended. The batter will be very thin and pourable, like thin pancake batter.

Pour the batter into the oiled pan. Shake the pan gently to level the batter out to the sides.

Bake for 33 – 36 minutes.
The top will spring back when gently pressed. The surface will be quite firm, and the edges may even be a little crispy, pulling away from the pan sides. Cool it in the pan on a rack. Allow it to cool quite a bit before cutting it into squares or bars.

MOCHA FUDGE COFFEE CAKE
(WHEAT-FREE)

Makes 16–20 pieces

For chocolate lovers, this stuff is irresistible!

Preheat oven to 375°.
Oil a 9 inch round or 8 inch square baking pan; dust it with cocoa powder.

1/4 cup raspberry or strawberry preserves,
    fruit-sweetened

1 cup brown rice flour
1 cup quinoa flakes
1/2 cup egg replacer powder
3/8 cup cocoa powder
1/4 cup powdered coffee substitute
1/2 tablespoon baking powder
1/2 tablespoon baking soda

1/2 cup unrefined sugar
1/2 cup soymilk
1/3 cup vegan sour cream
1/4 cup applesauce
2 tablespoons canola oil
2 tablespoons vanilla extract

1/4 cup boiling water

Stir the preserves in a small cup to make them more "runny."

Sift together the rice flour, quinoa, egg replacer powder, cocoa, coffee substitute, baking powder and baking soda.

In a food processor, use the knife blade to process together the sugar, soymilk, vegan sour cream, applesauce, oil and vanilla. Add the rice flour mixture to the processor in two portions. Process the ingredients together each time until they are well-combined.
Pour the boiling water through the tube into the processor while it is running. Run it just until all the ingredients are fully combined, and the batter is lump-free. It will be very pourable.

Immediately pour the batter into the baking pan, leveling it out to the sides.
Drop blobs of the preserves on the top and swirl them back and forth across the surface with a knife or spatula.
Put it in the oven right away.

Bake 27-30 minutes.
The surface will be firm and shiny. A cake tester will come out clean. Cool it in the pan on a rack for 10 minutes. Gently loosen it and remove it from the pan. (Before inverting it, place a piece of waxed paper over the top to keep the molten preserves from sticking to you or a paper towel. Remove the waxed paper after you turn it right-side-up.) Allow it to mostly cool on the rack before slicing it.

OATMEAL BREAKFAST CAKE

Makes 12–16 pieces

Preheat oven to 350°.
Prepare a 9 inch round or 8 inch square cake pan.

1/3 cup apricot preserves, fruit-sweetened

1 cup regular rolled oats
1 1/2 cups boiling water

1 cup whole wheat pastry flour
1/2 cup barley flour
1 teaspoon baking soda
1 teaspoon cinnamon
1/2 teaspoon nutmeg

3/8 cup apple or white grape juice
2 tablespoons egg replacer powder

3/8 cup light brown muscovado sugar
1/4 cup applesauce
2 tablespoons canola oil

Crunchy Nutty Topping (page 83)

Measure the preserves into a small bowl, and if necessary beat them with a fork to make them smoother and more liquefied.

Put the oats in a heat-resistant bowl and pour the boiling water over them. Stir them a little and set them aside to cool.

Sift together the flours, baking soda, cinnamon and nutmeg.

Whisk the egg replacer into the juice.
Beat it together with the sugar, applesauce and oil for 1-2 minutes, until very bubbly.
Beat in the soaked oats at medium speed until they are fully combined with the other ingredients.
Beat the flour mixture into the other ingredients at medium speed until everything is fully combined. The batter will be very thick and barely pourable.

Spread a little over half of the batter evenly in the baking pan. Level it out to the pan edges.
Spread the preserves evenly over this batter.
Spread the rest of the batter out to the edges of the pan. Cover the preserves completely and evenly.

Bake 45-48 minutes.
The top will be dark golden brown. It will spring back when lightly pressed.

MEANWHILE, prepare the Crunchy Nutty Topping. Follow the Topping directions to finish the cake. Allow it to cool completely before cutting it.

PUMPKIN SPICE TEABREAD

Makes 16-30 slices

Preheat oven to 350°.
Lightly oil two 8 1/2 x 4 1/2 inch loaf pans, or one 10 inch Bundt or tube pan.

3 cups unbleached pastry flour
1/2 cup stoneground whole wheat flour
2 1/4 teaspoons baking powder
2 teaspoons pumpkin pie spice
1 teaspoon baking soda

3/4 cup unrefined sugar
3/8 cup canola oil
1/4 cup light brown muscovado sugar
1/4 cup apple or white grape juice
2 teaspoons vanilla extract

1/4 cup apple or white grape juice
1 tablespoon egg replacer powder

1 1/2 cups pumpkin, cooked and pureed
2 teaspoons apple cider vinegar

1/4 cup soymilk (as needed)

Sift the flours, baking powder, spice and baking soda together.

Use a mixer to beat together the sugars, oil, 1/4 cup of juice and vanilla at high speed until the mixture is well-combined.

Whisk the egg replacer powder into the other 1/4 cup of juice. Beat it into the sugar mixture at medium speed until it is bubbly. Beat the pumpkin and vinegar into this mixture.
Beat the flour mixture into all the other ingredients in two portions, just until everything is well-combined. The batter should be like very thick cake batter, just barely pourable. If it is too thick (since pumpkin varies in wetness), add a little of the soymilk, as needed.

Pour half of the batter into each loaf pan, or all of it into the tube pan, leveling it out to the sides.

Bake 60-70 minutes (for loaf pans).
Bake 70-85 minutes (for a tube pan).
The surface will be a rich reddish brown. The top will spring back when lightly pressed. There will be a hollow sound when you lightly tap the surface. A cake tester will come out clean.

The loaves can be removed from their pans almost immediately. If you are using a tube pan, cool it in the pan on a rack for 15 minutes, then gently loosen the sides and remove the teabread. Allow it to finish cooling on a rack before slicing.

RAISIN MAPLE LOAF

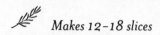

Makes 12–18 slices

Preheat oven to 350°.
Lightly oil and flour an 8 1/2 x 4 1/2 inch loaf pan.

2 1/4 cups unbleached pastry flour
1/2 tablespoon cinnamon
1 teaspoon baking powder
1/2 teaspoon nutmeg

3/4 cup water
1/2 cup raisins
1/2 teaspoon baking soda

1/4 cup white grape juice
2 tablespoons water
2 tablespoons egg replacer powder

3/8 cup maple syrup
2 tablespoons canola oil

Sift together the flour, cinnamon, baking powder and nutmeg.

Put the raisins and 3/4 cup of water in a small pan. Bring the raisins to a boil, remove them from the heat, and add the baking soda.

Stir together the juice and water. Whisk in the egg replacer powder.

Drain the water off the raisins and reserve the raisins.

Use a mixer to beat the egg replacer mixture, raisin water, syrup and oil together at high speed until they are frothy.

Add about 1 cup of the flour mixture and beat at high speed for 1 minute.

Add the rest of the flour mixture and beat it in at medium speed just until all the ingredients are fully combined.

Fold in the raisins at low speed or by hand.

Spread the batter evenly in the loaf pan.

Bake 30-35 minutes.

The loaf will turn golden brown. The top will spring back when gently pressed. A cake tester will come out clean. Allow it to cool 15-20 minutes in the pan on a rack. Then gently loosen the sides and turn it out onto the rack. Turn it right-side up to cool completely on the rack before slicing.

VERY EASY TEA CAKE

Makes 8-16 slices

This cake is not only easy but versatile. If you try all the options, you can make a couple dozen without repeating yourself! For a special dessert split a slice, lay the slices side-by-side, and top them with a scoop of frozen dessert and some fresh fruit!

Preheat oven to 325°.
Oil a 9 inch round or 8 inch square pan.

2 3/4 cups unbleached pastry flour
1/2 cup canola oil
Optional:
    1 teaspoon pumpkin pie spice or cinnamon
    OR 1/2 teaspoon cardamom or powdered ginger
    OR 1/4 teaspoon nutmeg or mace

1 cup soymilk
1/2 cup unrefined sugar
2 tablespoons apple cider vinegar
1 teaspoon baking soda
Optional:
    1 tablespoon vanilla extract
    OR 1 teaspoon lemon or orange extract
    OR 1/2 teaspoon mint or anise extract

Optional:
3/4 cup nuts
3/4 cup dairy-free chocolate chips

(Sift the spice into the flour.)
Rub the canola oil into the flour with a wooden spoon.

Use a mixer to beat together the soymilk, sugar, vinegar, baking soda (and flavoring) at high speed, until they are very bubbly. Pour this mixture into the flour mixture and beat everything together at high speed, just until they are fully combined. The batter will be smooth and pourable.
(Beat in the nuts and/or chips at low speed or by hand.)

Pour the batter into the pan and level it out to the sides.

Bake 35-45 minutes.
The top will spring back when gently pressed. A cake tester will come out clean. Cool it in its pan on a rack for 10 minutes. Carefully remove it and finish cooling it on the rack.

ZUCCHINI BREAD

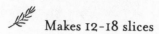 Makes 12-18 slices

Preheat oven to 350°.
Lightly oil and flour an 8 1/2 x 4 1/2 inch loaf pan.

1 cup zucchini, peeled and shredded*

1 cup stoneground whole wheat flour
1 cup unbleached pastry flour
1 tablespoon pumpkin pie spice
1/2 tablespoon baking powder
1 teaspoon baking soda

1/2 cup unrefined sugar
2 tablespoons canola oil
2 teaspoons lemon extract

1/4 cup apple juice
2 tablespoons apple cider vinegar
2 tablespoons water
2 tablespoons egg replacer powder

1/2 cup pecans or walnuts, chopped (optional)

1 teaspoon soymilk

Sift together the flours, spice, baking powder and baking soda.

Combine the sugar, oil and lemon extract in a large bowl.

Combine the apple juice, apple cider vinegar and water in a cup.
Whisk in the egg replacer powder.
Add this mixture to the sugar mixture. Beat everything together at high speed until it is bubbly.
Beat in the zucchini at medium-high speed.
Beat in the flour mixture at medium speed just until all of the ingredients are fully combined. The batter will be like a soft dough.
(Fold in the nuts at low speed.)

Spread the batter in the pan, leveling it out to the sides.
Dip your fingers in the soymilk, and use them to smooth out the surface of the batter.

Bake 40-45 minutes.
The top will be golden brown. A cake tester should come out clean. It will spring back when gently pressed. Cool it in the pan on a rack for 10-15 minutes before removing it. Allow it to finish cooling on the rack before slicing.

* For a very large zucchini, first slice it lengthwise into quarters. This will produce shorter shreds. Set the shredded zucchini in a colander while continuing other preparations. When you are ready to add it to the batter, wrap it in two layers of waxed paper, and squeeze and wring it out very firmly for a minute or less, to get as much excess juice out of it as possible.

CREAMY TOPPING

Makes about 1 1/4 cups

3/4 cup soy yogurt
1 tablespoon vanilla extract

3 tablespoons unrefined sugar
1 1/2 tablespoons cornstarch

1/2 cup soymilk
1 teaspoon canola oil

Stir the soy yogurt and vanilla together in a mixing bowl.

Stir together the sugar and cornstarch in a saucepan.
Gradually blend in the soymilk. Add the oil.
Cook the cornstarch mixture over medium-low heat for 4-5 minutes, until it becomes quite thick.
Add it to the soy yogurt mixture. Beat everything together until it is fully combined.

Keep this topping refrigerated until you are ready to serve it.

CRUNCHY NUTTY TOPPING

Makes about 3/4 cup

1/3 cup unbleached pastry flour
1/4 cup unrefined sugar
2 teaspoons cinnamon

1/4 cup soy yogurt
2 tablespoons canola oil

1/2 cup pecans or walnuts, chopped very small

WHILE the coffee cake is baking:
Stir together the flour, sugar and cinnamon.
Mix in the soy yogurt and oil with a fork, until all the ingredients are fully combined.
Stir in the chopped nuts.

As soon as the coffee cake is fully-baked, remove it from the oven.
Turn the oven up to "Broil."
Spread the topping evenly over the cake surface.
Put the cake in the broiler for exactly 1 minute; then check it.
The topping should be a tiny bit browned, and have formed a firm "crust." If not, give it 20 seconds more; check it again. If necessary, give it 10 or even 20 more seconds. Then remove it immediately. Allow it to cool for 15-20 minutes in its pan on a rack before trying to remove it. Cool it completely before cutting it.

FROZEN WHIPPED TOPPING

Makes about 3 cups

This stuff is not too sweet or fat-laden, and melts in a slow and satisfying way over whatever pastry onto which you scoop it. Two tablespoons is a reasonable serving.

1 (250 ml) container soy-based cream substitute*
1 teaspoon vanilla
1/8 teaspoon cream of tartar

1/2 cup unrefined sugar

Combine the cream substitute, vanilla and cream of tartar.
Pour in the sugar gradually, beating with a mixer at high speed.
Continue beating everything at high speed for 4-6 minutes.
The mixture will become frothy, with tinier and tinier bubbles.
As air is whipped into it, it will expand in volume until it reaches about 3 cups.
Scrape it into a plastic container with a lid and freeze it over-night.

* See Provamel, page 140.

LEMON SAUCE

Makes about 1 cup

This will keep in the refrigerator up to 2 weeks, and it reheats well.

1/4 cup unrefined sugar
1 tablespoon cornstarch

2 tablespoons lemon juice
1 tablespoon canola oil
1/2 cup water

1/2 cup water

1/2 teaspoon lemon extract

Stir the sugar and cornstarch together.
Gradually blend in the lemon juice until the cornstarch is completely dissolved.
Blend in the oil.
Stir in 1/2 cup of water.

Cook the mixture over medium heat, stirring constantly, until it begins to thicken.
Then add the other 1/2 cup of water.
Continue cooking and stirring until the whole surface is bubbling.

Remove the sauce from the heat and stir in the lemon extract.
You can serve this warm or cool.

VANILLA SAUCE

Makes about 1 cup

This will keep in the refrigerator up to 2 weeks.

I/4 cup unrefined sugar
I tablespoon cornstarch

I/4 cup vanilla soymilk

3/4 cup plain soy yogurt
4 teaspoons canola oil

I tablespoon vanilla extract

Stir the sugar and cornstarch together.
Gradually blend in the soymilk until the cornstarch dissolves completely.
Whisk in the soy yogurt and oil.

Cook this mixture over medium heat until it reaches a boil.
Turn the heat to low or medium-low, and allow the mixture to continue simmering for 10 minutes. Whisk it thoroughly about once a minute.

Then remove it from the heat and whisk in the vanilla.

SUGAR GLAZE

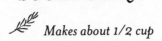 *Makes about 1/2 cup*

Have the pastry already baked and cooked.
Have your pastry brush wet and squeezed out.

1/2 cup unrefined sugar
2 tablespoons water
2 tablespoons soymilk (plain or vanilla)

1-4 tablespoons additional hot water, in a kettle

Optional:
1/2 teaspoon vanilla extract
1/4 teaspoon lemon extract

Combine the sugar, water and soymilk in a small saucepan.
Bring the mixture to a boil, stirring constantly with a heat-resistant spatula. Lower the heat and simmer the mixture for 4-5 minutes, stirring and scraping down the sides constantly. If the mixture begins to dry and crystallize too soon, add 1/2 tablespoon of water at a time, as needed.
(After 4 minutes, stir in the flavoring.)

As soon as you remove the glaze from the heat, use it.
Brush the glaze from the center out to the sides. It's okay if there are some drips down the sides. It will look decorative.

Allow the glaze to set before slicing the pastry. Refrigerating it for about 30 minutes will speed up the process.

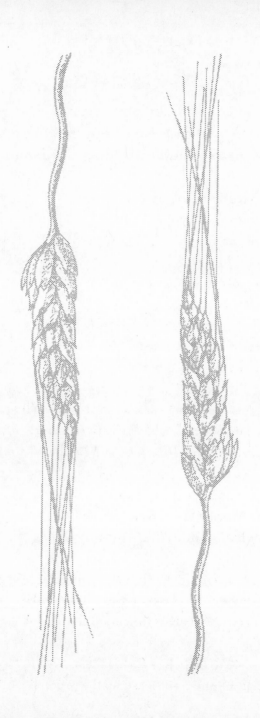

Three: Quick Breads

SOME THOUGHTS ON MAKING QUICK BREADS

While quick breads are a very broad category, to me a real quick bread has the most bread-like texture, and is not too sweet or "desserty." Also, they are more likely to be used as an accompaniment to an entrée, while muffins, coffee cakes, and teabreads function most often as a snack. Scones sort of sit on the fence, and I've chosen to include them here with biscuits and "baking pan" breads. One thing that all quick breads have in common is that they never used yeast (a "slow" leavening), and they bake very fast, at fairly high heats. The majority also require a little kneading.

Kneading

Kneading quick bread dough is not the same as kneading yeast dough. It has to be done with a light touch, and not for too long. I recommend a maximum of one minute for any of them — if you can get it done in thirty seconds, all the better. In fact, try not to think of it as kneading (with its pushing, pulling, and pounding connotations) at all. Think of it as beating, or even whisking, but on a floured board instead of in a bowl, and with your fingers instead of a whisk or beaters.

Your goal is to work just enough additional flour into your dough that you can handle and cut it easily. That's why you start with the board and dough generously floured. (Use a slotted spoon to sift flour layers about the thickness of corrugated cardboard.)

Stretch and spread the dough, letting the flour get in contact with as much sticky dough surface as possible. Push it back together, scrunch it, flip it. Keep your eye on the clock, and your fingers moving fast, as you keep repeating this process. If it's sticking a lot, sift on more flour.

When near the one-minute mark, push and scrunch the dough, forming one, two or three flattened disks. Start with a ball of dough, and press and push it down on a thin layer of flour. Work from the middle to the edges, making a disk of even thickness (usually from 1/2 -1 inch). When shaping smaller disks to cut into wedge-shaped scones, don't worry about perfect smoothness or geometrically-precise edges. You want a rustic, handmade look. That's part of their charm.

Cutting Them

For wedge-shaped scones, disks should be about 6-8 inches across. Cut each one into six pieces, with three crossways cuts like you're slicing a pie.

For cut-out biscuits or scones, the traditional shape is round. A standard biscuit cutter is 2 1/2 inches in diameter. This happens to be just about the width of the average drinking glass, which you can use if you don't have a cutter. With a glass, be sure to flour the edges well each time. Cutters are more or less open at top, so the dough usually doesn't get stuck.

But in a glass, the dough can form a small vacuum and keep the biscuit from just dropping out. Floured edges will help.

For the Surprise Scones, if you want to make cute little bite-size ones, use a cutter or glass under 2 inches in diameter. I won't get into the geometry of it, but it's amazing how much less dough a scone uses when you reduce its diameter by 1/2 or 3/4 of an inch.

Baking Them

When using baking soda, it is crucial to have the oven fully preheated *before* the items are ready to bake. Baking soda doesn't like to sit around and wait once it has been combined with liquids. It loses its vigor fast. Baking powder is a lot more patient.

You will find a couple of recipes for stovetop-baked scones. That method will actually work with any of the biscuits or scones, and is a useful technique when the weather is too hot to have the oven on high. They won't rise quite as much this way, but will still be tender and delicious. You can also use this method to bake biscuits when camping or cooking out. Stoves vary a lot, so watch them carefully, and adjust the burner as necessary, anywhere between simmer and low. Baking time may vary from three to six minutes per side.

Serving and Eating Them

Of course all quick breads are delightful warm from the oven, but all are also delicious cold or reheated. They also freeze well. Thaw them out in a toaster oven.

My feeling about scones is that they exist to be split open and spread with things. Other people just spread something on top, and still others eat them "au naturel." There really isn't any wrong way. Only not eating them would be wrong!

BANANA STOVETOP SCONES

 *Makes 8-12*

This is a somewhat unconventional flavor for scones, but it works beautifully!

Heat one or two cast iron skillets or griddles on the stove top at the lowest heat.

Be sure you have lids available that will fit them.

Have a can of canola oil cooking spray handy.

Have your kneading board ready, generously floured.

1/3 cup soymilk
1 tablespoon apple cider vinegar

2 cups unbleached pastry flour
1 tablespoon baking soda
1/4 teaspoon nutmeg

1 large ripe banana, mashed
1 1/2 tablespoons canola oil
1-2 tablespoons honey or other liquid sweetener

Stir the vinegar into the soymilk.

Sift together the flour, baking soda and nutmeg. Make a "well" in the middle of the flour.

Stir the oil and sweetener into the mashed banana.
Pour the mixture into the "well." Use a fork to stir everything together quickly, just until all the ingredients are combined. The dough should start pulling away from the bowl, and not look wet anywhere.

Turn the dough out onto your kneading board. Sift a layer of flour over the surface. Knead quickly and lightly for just one minute.
As you finish the kneading process, divide the dough into two portions, and form each into a flattened disk about 1/2 inch thick. Use a sharp knife to cut each one into four or six wedges.

Put as many wedges onto each of the hot skillets as you can fit, about 1 inch apart. Cover the skillets with the lids.

Bake the scones on one side for 2-3 minutes.
They should be lightly browned on the undersides. Keep an eye on them — they get dark very fast. They will puff up somewhat.
Turn them, cover and bake them for another 2-3 minutes.
They should be lightly browned on the second sides. Check the cut edges to make sure they are done through. If the cut edges look and feel doughy, give the scones another minute on the least-brown side.

When the first batch is baked, put on the rest and repeat the process.

BUTTERMILK-STYLE BISCUITS

Makes 9-12

Preheat oven to 450°.
Place a large unoiled baking sheet on the middle rack of the oven to preheat.
Have your kneading board ready, generously floured.

2 cups unbleached pastry flour
2 teaspoons baking powder
1 teaspoon baking soda

1/4 cup canola oil (very cold)

1/2 cup soymilk, less 1 tablespoon (very cold)
1/4 cup soy yogurt (very cold)
1 tablespoon apple cider vinegar

additional flour for kneading

Sift the flour, baking powder and baking soda together.

Rub the oil into the flour mixture. Start with a wooden spoon and after it is mostly combined, finish rubbing it in with your fingers. The texture should be like fine bread crumbs. Make a "well" in the middle.

Combine the soymilk, soy yogurt and vinegar. Use a glass or clear plastic liquid measuring cup. First, measure in the soy yogurt. Add the vinegar. Then pour in the soymilk, up to the 3/4 cup line. Stir these all together.

Pour the soymilk mixture into the "well." Use a fork to mix all the ingredients together, just until they are fully combined. The dough will be like wet bread dough.

Turn the dough out on your floured board. Sift a layer of flour over the top of the dough. Knead the dough quickly and lightly, sifting more flour as necessary, for just one minute.

As you finish kneading the dough, press and pat it out into a large disk about 3/4 inch thick.

Place all the biscuits about one inch apart on the hot baking sheet in the oven.

Bake 10-12 minutes.
They will puff up and become golden. Serve these hot.

CELTIC SODA BREAD

Makes 4 huge or 8 generous wedges; 20-24 hearty slices

This versatile bread works wonderfully as an accompaniment to soups and stews, sliced for sandwiches, or broken and spread with fruit preserves. Traditionally this kind of bread was made with buttermilk or sour milk. Vinegar and soy yogurt serve the same purpose — providing acid to react with the baking soda and make the dough rise.

Preheat oven to 400°.
Lightly oil a cast iron skillet, cake pan or pie plate.
Have your kneading board ready, generously floured.

2 cups unbleached pastry flour
2 cups stoneground whole wheat flour
2 tablespoons unrefined sugar (optional)
4 teaspoons baking soda
1 teaspoon cardamom (optional)

3/4 cup soymilk
3/4 cup soy yogurt
2 tablespoons canola oil
2 teaspoons apple cider vinegar

Sift the flours, (sugar), baking soda (and cardamom) together. Make a "well" in the flour mixture.

Use a fork to lightly beat the soymilk, soy yogurt, oil and vinegar together.

Pour this mixture into the "well." Use the fork to mix all the ingredients together rapidly. Don't worry if the flour is not completely blended in.

Turn the dough out immediately onto the floured board. Knead it quickly and lightly for just one minute. As you knead, work in any loose scraps of dough or pockets of flour. The dough will be a little sticky, but it will hold together well.

As you finish the kneading, form the dough into a round loaf. Flatten it slightly as you place it in the skillet. DON'T push and press it out to the edges — let it sit there with a little air space around it.

Use a sharp knife to make two deep cuts at right angles straight across the loaf, nearly to the bottom of the dough. Put the bread into the oven immediately.

Bake at 400° for 20 minutes.
Turn the oven down to 375° and bake for 10 minutes more. The bread will be golden brown. It will have a hollow sound when you tap the top. Serve it warm or cool.

CHOCOLATE SCONES

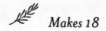

Makes 18

Preheat oven to 375°.
Place a large, unoiled baking sheet on the middle rack
of the oven to preheat.
Have your kneading board ready, generously floured.

2 cups spelt flour
1/4 cup cocoa powder
1/4 cup unrefined sugar
1 teaspoon baking powder
1 teaspoon baking soda

2 tablespoons canola oil
2 teaspoons vanilla extract

1/2 cup soy yogurt
1/2 cup chocolate soymilk

Sift together the flour, cocoa powder, sugar, baking powder and baking soda.

Rub the canola oil and vanilla extract into the flour mixture. Start with a wooden spoon, and then your fingers, until the flour has a texture like cornmeal. Form a "well" in the center of the flour mixture.

Stir together the soy yogurt and soymilk. Pour this mixture into the flour "well."
Use a fork to rapidly beat all the ingredients together just until they are fully combined.
Turn the dough out onto the floured kneading board. Sift a layer of flour over the top of the dough. Knead the dough quickly and lightly for just one minute.
Finish the kneading process by dividing the dough into three portions, and forming each into a flattened disk 3/4 inch thick. Use a sharp knife to cut each one into six wedges.

Place all the wedges about 1 inch apart on the hot baking sheet in the oven.

Bake 11-13 minutes.
They will puff up. They should have a slight hollow sound when tapped. If you're in any doubt, test the doneness by breaking one open. Remove them from the baking sheet to a rack. Serve them warm or cold.

CORNBREAD

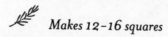 *Makes 12–16 squares*

This cornbread is quick, reliable and delicious — a great addition to your baking repertoire!

Preheat oven to 400°.
Lightly oil an 8 x 8 inch baking pan.

I 1/2 cups stoneground whole wheat flour
I cup + 2 tablespoons cornmeal
I 1/2 tablespoons unrefined sugar
1/2 tablespoon baking soda

5 tablespoons water
I 1/2 tablespoons egg replacer powder

I cup soymilk
3 tablespoons canola oil
2 tablespoon apple cider vinegar

I-2 teaspoons soymilk (for top)

Sift together the cornmeal, flour, sugar and baking soda.

Whisk the egg replacer powder into the water.
Combine it with the soymilk, oil and vinegar.
Use a mixer to beat these ingredients together at high speed until the mixture is very bubbly.
Beat in the cornmeal mixture at medium-high speed just until all the ingredients are fully combined.

Spread the batter in the pan, leveling it out to the edges.
Dip your fingers in the soymilk, and use them to smooth out the surface of the batter.

Bake 20-25 minutes.
The surface will be golden brown and crusty. The top will spring back when gently pressed. A cake tester or knife will come out clean. Leave it in the pan. You can cut and serve this warm or cold.

HERBED SPELT SQUARES

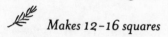

Makes 12–16 squares

Like cornbread, these fit somewhere between biscuits and breads, and can function in either capacity. They make a wonderful complement to baked beans, soups, and stews. And the cold leftover squares make lovely little sandwiches — split them horizontally.

Preheat oven to 450°.
Lightly oil an 8 x 8 inch baking pan.

1 3/4 cups spelt flour
2 teaspoons baking powder
1 teaspoon baking soda

1/4 cup canola oil (very cold)

3/4 cup soymilk (very cold)
1 tablespoon apple cider vinegar
1-2 tablespoon dried herbs
    OR 2-3 tablespoons fresh herbs, chopped fine
ground pepper, to taste

Sift the flour, baking powder and baking soda together.

Rub the oil into the flour mixture thoroughly. Start the process with a wooden spoon. After it is fairly well worked in, switch to using your fingers. The texture should be like fine bread crumbs. Make a "well" in the middle of the mixture.

Use a fork to stir together the soymilk, vinegar, herbs and pepper.

Pour this mixture into the "well." Use the fork to quickly stir all the ingredients together, just until they are fully combined. The dough will be soft, sticky, and a little bubbly.

Scrape all the dough into the pan. Spread it out as level as possible to the edges.
Put it into the oven immediately.

Bake 10-12 minutes.
The surface will be golden and crusty. It will spring back slightly when gently pressed. Serve it hot, warm, or cold.

LEMON SCONES

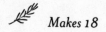

Makes 18

Preheat oven to 375°.
Place a large, unoiled baking sheet on the middle rack
of the oven to preheat.
Have your kneading board ready, generously floured.

2 1/4 cups Kamut flour
1/4 cup unrefined sugar
I teaspoon baking powder
I teaspoon baking soda

2 tablespoons canola oil
1/2 teaspoon lemon extract

1/2 cup soy yogurt
1/3 cup lemon juice
1/4 cup soymilk

Sift together the flour, sugar, baking powder and baking soda.

Rub the canola oil and lemon extract into the flour mixture. Start with a wooden spoon, and then your fingers, until the flour has a texture like cornmeal. Form a "well" in the center of the flour mixture.

Stir together the soy yogurt, lemon juice and soymilk. Pour this mixture into the flour "well."
Use a fork to rapidly beat this mixture into the flour mixture, just until all the ingredients are combined.
Turn the dough out onto the floured kneading board. Sift some additional flour over the top of the dough. Knead the dough quickly and lightly for just one minute.

As you finish the kneading process, divide the dough into three portions, and form each into a flattened disk about 3/4 inch thick. Use a sharp knife to cut each one into six wedges.

Place all the wedges about 1 inch apart on the hot baking sheet in the oven.

Bake 11-13 minutes.
They will puff up and turn golden brown. They should have a slight hollow sound when tapped. Remove them from the baking sheet to a rack. Serve them warm or cold.

OAT SCONES

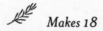 *Makes 18*

These are crusty on the outside, tender on the inside, and not very sweet — perfect to split and spread with preserves!

Preheat oven to 425°.
Place a large unoiled baking sheet on the middle rack of the oven to preheat.
Have your kneading board ready, generously floured.

5/8 cup soymilk
1 1/2 tablespoons apple cider vinegar
1/2 teaspoon lemon or orange extract (optional)

2 1/4 cups unbleached pastry flour
   OR 2 cups spelt flour
1 1/2 cups quick rolled oats (not instant)
1 1/2 tablespoons unrefined sugar
1/2 tablespoon cream of tartar
3/4 teaspoon baking soda

3 tablespoons canola oil
1 1/2 tablespoons apple or lemon juice

Stir the vinegar (and flavoring) into the soymilk.

Sift together the flour, oats, sugar, cream of tartar and baking soda.
Add the oil and apple juice. Use a wooden spoon to rub them into the flour mixture. The texture should become like fine bread crumbs. Make a "well" in the middle of the mixture.
Pour in the soymilk mixture. Use a fork to rapidly beat this into the flour mixture, just until all the ingredients are combined.

Turn the dough out onto the floured kneading board. Sift some additional flour over the top of the dough. Knead the dough quickly and lightly for just one minute.
Finish the kneading process by dividing the dough into three portions. Form each into a flattened disk about 1/2 inch thick. Use a sharp knife to cut each one into six wedges.

Place all the wedges about 1 inch apart on the hot baking sheet in the oven.

Bake 12-14 minutes.
They will puff up and turn light gold. They should have a slight hollow sound when tapped. Remove them from the baking sheet to a rack. Serve them warm or cold.

OLD-FASHIONED SCONES

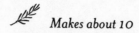

Makes about 10

If the oven is on at a high temperature for something else, this is a way to get some extra use out of the stored heat. Measure everything in advance, and whip these up just before your other baking is to come out.

Preheat oven to 425°.
Place a large baking sheet in the oven to preheat.
Have your kneading board ready, generously floured.

1 1/2 cups unbleached pastry flour
1 tablespoon unrefined sugar (optional)
1 rounded teaspoon cream of tartar
1 rounded teaspoon baking soda
1/2 teaspoon allspice

1 1/2 tablespoons canola oil

1/2 cup soymilk
1/2 tablespoon vinegar

Optional:
1/4 cup raisins or currants
plus 2 tablespoons very hot water
1/4 cup walnuts, chopped

additional flour for kneading

(Soak the raisins or currants in the hot water.)

Sift together the flour, (sugar), cream of tartar, baking soda and allspice.

Rub the oil into the flour mixture. Start with a wooden spoon and after it is mostly combined, finish rubbing it in with your fingers. The texture should be like fine bread crumbs. Make a "well" in the middle of the flour mixture.

Stir the vinegar into the soymilk. Pour the soymilk (and raisins and/or nuts) into the "well." Use a fork to mix all the ingredients together, just until they are fully combined. The dough will be like wet bread dough.

Scrape the dough out onto the floured board. Sift more flour over the top. Knead the dough rapidly for just one minute. The dough should become more elastic and much less sticky. Finish the kneading process by forming the dough quickly into flattened disk about 3/4 inch thick.

Use a standard biscuit cutter to cut scones. Gather up the excess dough, briefly re-knead it, and pat it out again. Cut as many more scones as possible.

Place the whole batch of scones about 1 inch apart on the hot baking sheet in middle of the oven.
TURN THE OVEN OFF.

Bake 10 minutes.
Do not open the oven door until the time is up. They will puff up and turn golden brown. Remove them to a rack to cool.

POTATO-RICE BISCUITS
(WHEAT-FREE)

 *Makes about 12*

These make an excellent accompaniment for soups and stews. Of course, without any gluten they will not rise much; however, they are surprisingly tender inside, and have a wonderful flavor.

Preheat oven to 375°.
Place a large baking sheet in the oven to preheat.
Have your kneading board ready, generously floured with brown rice flour.

1/2 cup (about 1 small) onion, minced
1 teaspoon canola oil
hot water as needed

1 cup instant mashed potato flakes
5/8 cup brown rice flour
1/4 cup buckwheat flour
1/4 cup quinoa flour
1/2 teaspoon baking powder
1/2 teaspoon baking soda
1/2-1 teaspoon multiple-seasoning blend

2 tablespoons canola oil

1 cup soymilk
2 tablespoons vegan sour cream, mashed
1 tablespoon apple cider vinegar

Sauté the onion in the canola oil until it is translucent. If the pan begins to dry, add a little hot water as necessary.

Sift together the potato flakes, rice, buckwheat and quinoa flours, baking powder, baking soda, and seasonings. Rub the canola oil into this mixture with a wooden spoon until it disappears, and the ingredients develop a somewhat crumbly appearance. Make a "well" in the middle of the mixture.

Stir together the soymilk, mashed vegan sour cream and vinegar. Pour this mixture and the cooked onion into the "well." Use a fork to stir all the ingredients together quickly, just until they are fully combined.

Turn the dough out on your floured board. Sift some more rice flour over the top of the dough. Knead the dough quickly and lightly for just one minute, using enough rice flour so that it is easy to handle. As you finish kneading the dough, press and pat it out into a large disk about 1/2 inch thick.
Use a standard biscuit cutter to cut biscuits. Gather up the excess dough, briefly re-knead it, and pat it out again. Cut as many more biscuits as possible.

Place all the biscuits about one inch apart on the hot baking sheet in the oven.

Bake 17-18 minutes.
They will be pale brown. The surfaces will be firm and crusty; they will not spring back. Remove them to a rack.

STOVETOP SCONES

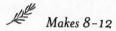 *Makes 8-12*

These are wonderful served warm from the griddle. Split them open and spread them with preserves. They're also fine cold or reheated.

Heat one or two cast iron skillets or griddles on the stove top at the lowest heat. *
Be sure you have lids available that will fit them.
Have a can of canola oil cooking spray handy.
Have your kneading board ready, generously floured.

1/2 cup soymilk
1 tablespoon apple cider vinegar

2 cups unbleached pastry flour
2 tablespoons unrefined sugar (optional)
1 tablespoon baking soda
1/2 teaspoon allspice (optional)

3 tablespoons canola oil
1 tablespoon honey or other liquid sweetener

* Make sure the skillet is a good temperature by dropping in a drop of water. If it sizzles and evaporates away quickly, it's probably about right. If it just sits there, it's not hot enough. And if it skitters and jumps around like crazy, the skillet is way too hot.

Stir the vinegar into the soymilk.

Sift together the flour (sugar) baking soda (and allspice). Make a "well" in the middle of the flour mixture.

Heat the oil and sweetener together in a small pan. When they are quite warm (not boiling) pour them into the "well."
Add the soymilk mixture. Use a fork to stir all the ingredients together quickly, making a soft dough. It should tend to pull away from the bowl, and not look wet anywhere.

Turn the dough out onto your kneading board. Sift a layer of flour over the surface. Knead quickly and lightly for just one minute. As you finish the kneading process, form the dough into two flattened disks about 1/2 inch thick. Use a sharp knife to cut each one into four or six wedges.

Put as many wedges onto each of the hot skillets as you can fit, about 1 inch apart. Cover the skillets with the lids.

Bake the scones on one side for 2-3 minutes.
They should be lightly browned on the undersides. Keep an eye on them — they get dark very fast. They will puff up somewhat. Turn them, cover and bake them for another 2-3 minutes.
 They should be lightly browned on the second sides. Check the cut edges to make sure they are done through. If the cut edges look and feel doughy, give the scones another minute on the least-brown side.

When the first batch is baked, put on the rest and repeat the process.

SURRISE SCONES

Makes 8–10 large, 18–20 small

Preheat oven to 375°.
Place a large, unoiled baking sheet in the oven to pre-heat.
Have your kneading board ready, generously floured.
Have your pastry brush wet and squeezed out.

2 cups unbleached pastry flour
1 tablespoon egg replacer powder
1 teaspoon baking powder
1/2 teaspoon baking soda

1/2 cup almond butter
1/4 cup unrefined sugar
2 tablespoons canola oil

3/8 cup soymilk
1/4 cup apple juice
1 tablespoon apple cider vinegar
1/2 teaspoon vanilla extract
1/2 teaspoon almond extract

5 teaspoons unsweetened fruit preserves
   OR several chocolate chips per scone

1-2 tablespoons soymilk for sealing the rounds together

For tops: 1-2 teaspoons unrefined sugar (optional)

Sift together the flour, egg replacer powder, baking powder and baking soda.

In a food processor, blend the almond butter, sugar and oil. Add the flour mixture to this. Process them together until they are completely blended and crumbly.

Add the soymilk, apple juice, vinegar, vanilla and almond extracts to the processor. Process in short pulses until the ingredients begin to clump together as a dough.

Scrape the dough out onto the floured board. Sift more flour over the top. Knead the dough rapidly for just thirty seconds. The dough should become easier to handle. Finish the kneading process by flattening the dough out to between 1/4 inch and 1/2 inch thick.

Cut out an even number of rounds.* Gather up the excess dough, briefly re-knead it, and pat it out again. Cut out more scones, using as much dough as possible.

Dip your pastry brush in the extra soymilk and lightly wet the whole top of *half* of the rounds. Drop 1/4 to 1/2 teaspoon of preserves in the middle of each of these. Cover these rounds with the others. Gently squeeze the edges together to seal them. Brush the tops with soymilk. (Sprinkle on a pinch of sugar.)

Bake 13-16 minutes.
They will puff up and be light brown all over. Cool them on a wire rack.

TOMATO BISCUITS

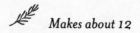 *Makes about 12*

These are very light and flaky — just don't over-knead them!

Preheat oven to 450°.
Place a large unoiled baking sheet on the middle rack of the oven to preheat.
Have your kneading board ready, generously floured.

2 cups unbleached pastry flour, unsifted
2 teaspoons baking powder
I teaspoon baking soda

I/4 cup canola oil, very cold

3/4 cup tomato juice, very cold
    OR tomato-based vegetable juice, very cold

additional flour for kneading

Sift the flour, baking powder and baking soda together.

Thoroughly rub the oil into the flour mixture with a wooden spoon. The texture should be like bread crumbs. Make a "well" in the middle of the mixture.

Pour in the juice. Use a fork to mix all the ingredients together quickly and lightly, just until they are fully combined. The dough will be soft and sticky, and a little bubbly.

Turn the dough out on your floured board. Sift a layer of flour over the top of the dough. Knead it quickly and lightly, sifting more flour as necessary, for just one minute. It should be easy to handle, and not very sticky.

As you finish kneading the dough, press and pat it out into a large disk between 1/2 and 3/4 inch thick. Use a standard biscuit cutter to cut biscuits. Gather up the excess dough, briefly re-knead it, and pat it out again. Cut a few more biscuits. You might do this once more to use as much dough as possible.

Place all the biscuits about one inch apart on the hot baking sheet in the oven.

Bake 10-12 minutes.
Serve these hot.

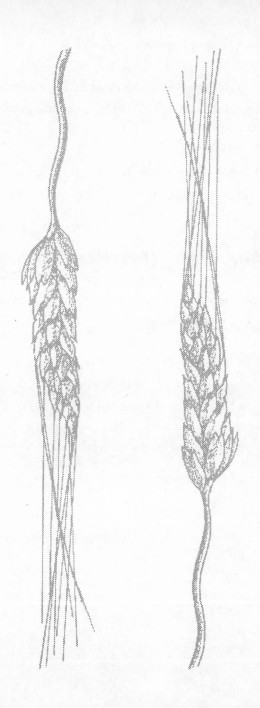

Four:
Baker's Support

USEFUL METHODS AND TECHNIQUES

Egg replacer powder, to mix and use

I like to mix this up in a one-cup glass measuring cup. Measure the liquid into the cup first. Then add the egg replacer powder. Whisk it into the liquid vigorously, using a small whisk.

Egg replacer can be used with plain water or fruit juice. Sometimes there are small lumps that don't dissolve, but I find that once I beat it into the other ingredients the lumps disappear — or at least don't show. In some recipes it gets sifted into the other dry ingredients.

Because the brand I buy comes in a cardboard box with a stiff paper inner pouch that is hard to re-seal, I have a glass jar with a screw-on lid, to which I transfer the powder. I store it with all my other non-refrigerated baking ingredients. This saves a lot of time.

Electric mixer, to beat with

No matter what speed is suggested for any step in the recipe, always start at the lowest setting, and gradually increase the speed as the ingredients are blended. This prevents explosive spattering.

Remember to stop and scrape down the sides of the bowl a few times during the process.

"All ingredients fully combined" means just until you don't see any little pockets of plain flour anywhere, and no excessively wet, runny patches. (This also goes for hand beating.)

Flour, to sift

All the flour measurements are for sifted flour, unless the recipe actually specifies unsifted.

I know there are objects called flour sifters out there in the world, but I have always just used a big slotted metal spoon. It allows me to reach down into the flour bag and do the initial sifting right there. Then I use it to scoop the flour out into the measuring cup, and again to sift all the dry ingredients together.

To sift in the bag, jiggle the spoon back and forth horizontally, until all the flour sifts through. Do this several times. This aerates the flour as much as necessary. For sifting ingredients together, dig the spoon down to the bottom of the bowl each time. Watch the colors in what you are sifting. As long as you can see streaks of different shades, you know the ingredients aren't completely integrated.

Lemon or orange peel, to grate

Wash the fruit, scrubbing with a vegetable brush. Air-dry or blot it. Cut off any discolored areas, and the stem-end.

Use the side of the grater with openings about as big around as the pointed end of a toothpick. Rest it on or over a plate or cutting board. Rub the fruit back and forth vigorously on the shredder, for only a second or two in any one area. As soon as the white pith begins to show, rotate to another area. Citrus that has had the outer peel removed like this can still be juiced.

Oil, to rub in by hand

The goal is to have the mixture look like very fine bread crumbs.

Always start with a wooden spoon. This saves a lot of mess. Once the oil is fairly well mingled with the flour, switch to using your hands. Rub any big, dark, oily clumps of flour together with dryer flour, between you thumb and other fingertips. If you have a big bowl, you can also use your palms.

Wheat-free flours, to bake with

Today more and more people seem to have either an allergy, or intolerance, to gluten. People with celiac disease, which is genetic, have a very severe gluten intolerance and must eliminate not only all forms of wheat (durum, semolina), but all also the alternative, "ancient" wheat flours (spelt, Kamut, farro, emmer and einkorn), and even all related grains (oats, barley, rye, triticale). These are all equally risky for people with such a sensitivity.* Recipes or cookbooks featuring these grains are not really eliminating gluten. This is something to keep in mind if you are baking for someone with a gluten-related health issue.

Yet some people may have only a mild (non-genetic) allergy, and can solve the problem using some of the "ancients,"

---

* This information was derived from *Prescription for Nutritional Healing*, by Balch & Balch, 2000, publisher Avery.

which appear to have different gluten. I use spelt and Kamut a lot, simply because they are flavorful. In general, spelt and Kamut are dryer than standard wheat flour, so if you wish to substitute them in a recipe calling for regular flour, I recommend reducing the total quantity by 1/8. For instance, for 1 cup of pastry flour, use 7/8 cup of spelt flour, for 2 cups of flour, use 1 3/4 cups of spelt flour, and so on.

People with a severe gluten intolerance absolutely must use alternative grains. Unfortunately, it is the gluten that is so effective in binding baked goods together. Eliminating gluten means being left with flours that don't hold together well! This in turn means combining them with other ingredients that have a binding, or sticky, quality. The most common alternative grains are rice, millet, corn and buckwheat. Less known but also gluten-free are quinoa and amaranth. It is also possible to bake with soy flour and potato flour. I've developed three good recipes here which use only gluten-free flours. A slightly dry texture is inescapable with these flours. My view is that if you are on a completely gluten-free diet, you have adjusted to the texture of these alternatives (or you're working on it). So I make no apologies for dryness. However, if you are not gluten-intolerant, and you find those recipes appealing enough to try, I recommend using unbleached pastry flour (increase the quantity by 2 tablespoons per cup).

A PERSONAL GUIDE
TO NATURAL INGREDIENTS

*This book was written using only the most natural, unrefined, and pref-
erably organic ingredients available. All these recipes worked very well
using the ingredients described here.*

*In the interest of space and simplicity, words such as "organic" and
"whole-grain" have been left out of the recipes. However, it is my hope
that you will want to maximize the healthfulness of these cookies, and use
the same types of natural ingredients that I use. In all cases, my recom-
mendation is organic, unrefined and non-GMO*.*

*So if you are new to the world of natural foods, I invite you to follow
my lead and stock your kitchen with these nutritious and flavorful ingredients. Here is a guide to help you on your journey of discovery.*

Apples

· Applesauce will help baked goods rise and adds sweetness.

· Cider vinegar, unfiltered, is a well-known folk remedy for
lots of ailments, so it's good to add it to your diet. It reacts well
with baking soda to make baked goods rise. There is no vin-
egary taste after baking.

· Juice, unfiltered — being somewhat acidic, triggers a reaction
in baking soda. Being sweet, it reduces the need for sugar.

---

*GMO is the abbreviation for "genetically modified organism." This means a liv-
ing thing that cannot occur naturally. Many GMOs have genes spliced into them
from other species. For instance, GMO soybeans may have a nut gene that will
cause a reaction in people who are allergic to nuts. An even more Frankensteinian
splicing is that a spider gene has been introduced into some goats, so that a strong,
spider-silk-like fiber can be produced from their milk! For me, this conjures up
nightmarish images of goat-sized spiders with horns!

Canola oil

This is the healthiest oil for baking. Olive is very healthy, but would impart a strange taste to sweets. I use liquid canola oil, because hardened, hydrogenated vegetable oils are as unhealthy as animal fats. Much canola has been contaminated by cross-pollination from GMO canola.

Carob and chocolate

· Carob is a chocolate-like substance available as a powder or chips. It is a little fruitier in taste than chocolate (it reminds some people of dates added to chocolate). The powder or chips can be substituted for chocolate in my recipes.

· Chocolate chips — dairy-free ones will always be dark chocolate, because milk chocolate uses milk. They may be sweetened with unrefined sugar, grain or malt. Check to make sure there is no hydrogenated oil.

· Cocoa powder, unsweetened, is not the same as cocoa mix. This is cacao beans, ground into a powder. Look for a "fair trade" label on chocolate products, because a lot of big chocolate companies import cacao from Africa's Ivory Coast, where the plantations use mostly child slave labor.

Coffee substitute, grain-based

There are a number of brands of powdered, coffee-like beverages. I don't drink coffee because that much caffeine is bad for my nerves and temper. There is also evidence that caffeine increases uterine fibroids and breast cysts.

Dairy substitutes, soy-based

· Cream substitute is like soymilk, but thicker and creamier. It won't whip up into peaks like dairy cream, but it does whip into a froth. I've only found one brand, which comes in sterile 250 ml boxes. (See Provamel, page 136.)

• Soy yogurt is fermented with the same types of helpful lacto-bacilli as in dairy yogurt. It works well in baked goods that call for buttermilk.

You can substitute an equal amount of soymilk, PLUS 1 teaspoon of apple cider vinegar per 1/2 cup of soymilk.

• Soymilk is available both plain and flavored. Try to find one enriched with Vitamin B12 (which vegans need to include in their diets).

• Soymilk powder is dried soymilk.

• Tofu (silken) is available in a sterile package that can be stored on a shelf, without refrigeration. It is extremely smooth and creamy in texture, and mild in flavor. It is often used in baking as a substitute for sour cream, heavy cream, or cream cheese.

• Vegan sour cream looks more like sour cream than tastes like it, but I've found it to be very useful for binding baked goods, and making them light and tender.

• Other types of nondairy milks include nut milks, rice milk and oat milk. These are all good for you and have varying types of enrichment. If you prefer them, by all means use them. I like soy because it has virtually eliminated my hot flashes.

Flavorings and extracts

If you can't find organic ones, at least avoid artificial flavorings, which are made with all sorts of chemicals.

Some brands are made with oil, and have to be refrigerated once opened. Alcohol-based ones can sit on a shelf. The actual alcohol is evaporated by heat, of course.

My baking philosophy is to cut back on added sweeteners and oil, and increase the flavor. So you may be surprised at the recommended amounts of flavorings (and spices as well) in this cookbook.

Flours

• Barley is actually in the wheat family, and has gluten. It is very flavorful in baked goods.

• Brown rice is useful for people who have a gluten allergy. However, the lack of gluten makes it tricky to use in baked goods.

• Kamut® is a "rediscovered" type of wheat which seems to be similar to early domesticated forms, possibly from Mesopotamia. People who have a mild gluten allergy can sometimes tolerate Kamut and/or spelt. Apparently the gluten is chemically different.

• Millet, see brown rice.

• Spelt probably originated in Europe about 7,000 years ago. See Kamut.

• Stoneground whole wheat is made from hard red winter wheat. It has a lot of gluten, which produces that spongy, fibrous texture in bread.

• Unbleached pastry flour is made from soft white spring wheat. It has less gluten, so it produces lighter, less-dense baked goods.

Fruit, dried

I like to use dried fruit in baking, since its sweetness reduces the need to add other sweeteners. Organically-grown is quite available now. However, a lot of dried fruit is preserved with sulfur dioxide. You can usually tell the sulfured fruit, because it is much more plump and juicy and light-colored than unsulfured dried fruit (which often looks like it has been lying in the road for a couple of weeks).

Health food wisdom says that you should avoid ingesting sulfur dioxide. I must confess that I buy some types of sulfured fruit anyway, because the other stuff looks so unappetizing. There are always trade-offs. If you focus on the bottom line — the total amount of unhealthy substances you ingest — and the total isn't large, then you might as well occasionally slip up. You will no doubt live longer slipping up and having faith in your immune system, than tormenting yourself with fear and worry during every waking hour.

• Dates do not seem to ever be preserved with anything. Inspect them as you cut them open to remove the pits, because very occasionally there are insect eggs or larvae inside. They are easy to see; the whole inside surface will be covered. Finding one or two doesn't mean the whole package will be infested. I find far fewer now that I buy organic.

• Figs — none of my recipes include figs, because I just don't like them. Feel free to substitute figs for dates if you like figs.

• Pineapple preserved with fruit juice is available.

• Raisins without preservatives look and taste excellent. Some organic brands incorporate a small amount of canola or sunflower oil. I prefer oil-free.

Grains and starches, miscellaneous

• Amaranth is gluten-free. It is pretty expensive, and I don't really use it.

• Cornmeal — the blue kind seems to be more finely-ground, and not have the slight grittiness of the yellow cornmeal. It also seems a little sweeter to me. It has no gluten.

• Oats are nutritious. However, being in the wheat family, they contain gluten. Rolled oats have been flattened out while softened. Many grains are rolled ("flaked") this way now. The rolling breaks up the tougher outer hull, so flattened-out grains cook a lot faster than the intact versions. When my recipes call for rolled oats, I mean this kind. Quick oats are younger and smaller, or have been cut up into smaller pieces. Instant oatmeal is ground fine, and usually pre-cooked. None of my recipes use it.

• Potato flakes (instant mashed potatoes) do not have gluten. I haven't yet found an organic brand of instant mashed potatoes. At least be sure to get a brand that is nothing but potato, with maybe a little citric acid as a preservative.

• Quinoa originated in South America, and has been used for centuries by native people there. It is gluten-free.

Grape juice, white

This is a good sweetener. I use white rather than red because it has a milder flavor, and doesn't affect the color of the finished product.

Opened bottles of white grape juice tend to develop mold faster than most other juices. If it's been in the fridge for a couple of weeks, hold the bottle up and look at the bottom for cloudy, ball-shaped stuff. If you see it, don't use the juice.

Leavenings

• Baking powder is partly heat-activated (not chemically, like baking soda). I only recommend the aluminum-free type, because research shows a link between Alzheimer's disease and aluminum in the diet.

• Baking soda causes baked goods to rise by producing bubbles when it is combined with liquid acidic ingredients (such as fruit juices, or vinegar). It loses that energy quite fast, so the items need to get into the oven quickly.

Baking soda is mined out of the ground. So be skeptical if someone claims to be selling "organic" baking soda. However, you might prefer getting it from a company that does not do animal testing.*

· Cream of tartar is an acidic, crystallized substance derived from grape juice. It is a common component of baking powder, but can be purchased separately.

· Egg replacer powder mimics the rising and binding properties of eggs in baked goods. It is not possible to make meringue with it. I find that I get the best results by using one tablespoon of powder combined with 2 tablespoons of liquid as a per-egg substitute.

Nuts and nut butters

Every popular variety of nut is now being organically-grown. You can also find many organic nut butters.

None of my recipes use peanuts or peanut butter. Peanuts go rancid very easily. Rancid peanuts contain aflatoxin, a carcinogen. I suspect that mainstream brands of peanut butter add chemicals and flavorings to cover up any taste of rancidity. If you must have peanuts, try to buy organically-grown ones, and either buy natural brands of peanut butter without additives, or make your own in a food processor.

* According to the National Anti-Vivisection Society, Arm & Hammer does test on animals.

Sea salt

Salt can cause high blood pressure. I only use salt in yeast breads. I think desserts don't need to be salty. But if you must, do use sea salt in very small amounts.

Spices

There are many organically-grown spices available now. Pumpkin pie spice is a blend of a number of spices. I like its balanced spicy flavor, and it saves some measuring time.

Sugars, granulated

• Birch Sugar (xylitol) is a new sweetener. It is white and crystalized, but does not involve charred animal bones. The texture makes it a useful one-to-one substitute for cane sugar. Advantages include: half the calories of sugar, slow to metabolize, and it does not seem to bring on sugar-imbalance health conditions. It does not taste quite as sweet as sugar. *I have not had reliable results with it in baking.*

• Maple sugar, as far as I know, is just dried, crystallized maple syrup, and not refined. I have never gotten into using it, because it is quite pricey, and maple isn't one of my favorite flavors.

• Natural dark brown molasses sugar is unrefined cane juice, with the molasses left in. Mainstream brown sugars are made from white, highly-refined sugar, which then has molasses added back to it. Why would anybody do that? I have no idea.

• Natural light brown muscovado is like "natural dark brown molasses sugar," above, but not as intensely molasses-y.

• Powdered or confectioner's sugar is usually made from refined white sugar, ground up very fine, with cornstarch added.

Recently Rapunzel, Hain, and Trader Joe's have added organic versions to their product lists. They all perform just like mainstream brands. Rapunzel's is beige and definitely unbleached. Trader Joe's is whiter, and unbleached. Hain's is white, and the labeling is unclear.

• Unrefined cane sugar has gone straight from being (organic) raw sugar cane juice, to being dried and ground up. White, refined sugar has gone through cooking, filtering, and bleaching, which has reduced it to simple carbohydrates. Unrefined sugar has some nutrients and flavor, not just sweetness.

Surely the most unappealing aspect of refined white sugar is that charred animal bones are used in the bleaching process. Thus white sugar is unacceptable for vegetarians. In Europe, where there is much more honesty about bovine spongiform encephalopathy (BSE, or mad cow disease), many candy companies now use some type of "non-bone-char" sugar. BSE contaminants are usually found in brain and spinal column tissue, as well as blood and bone marrow. They cannot be destroyed by high heat. The first confirmed North American case has now turned up in Canada. This is probably much more information than you wanted; but if you are curious about the facts, check these websites: www.mad-cow.org; www.testcowsnow.com. Or call Physicians Committee for Responsible Medicine (202) 686-2210.

Sweeteners, liquid

• Brown rice syrup: This is made from cooked-down whole brown rice. There are several levels of sweetness available. The flavor is not too obtrusive. It is a reasonable substitute for honey in baked goods.

• Fruit sweetener: This is made from cooked-down, concentrated fruit juice. The flavor seems to work well in baked goods with a lot of fruit and spice. However, in my experience, it seems to produce a musty aftertaste in chocolate-flavored things.

• Honey: It is impossible to regulate where bees fly, so no honey can be labeled as coming from organic flowers. Organic honey means the bees haven't had drugs or antibiotics.

I recommend raw honey. That means the producer doesn't heat it to more than flow temperature. Unfiltered means that large foreign particles have been filtered out, but the pollen (which is healthful) is left in. People with plant allergies find that using pollen-laden honey has reduced or eliminated their allergic reactions.

Very strict vegans avoid honey, because it comes from animals. I have visited a small, family-owned honey farm, and I did not see bees being exploited, restrained, tortured, or slaughtered. So I use it. I only buy honey from small independent beekeepers, who take very good care of their bees and only take about 10% of each hive's total output. Those who are deeply disturbed by bee exploitation must also give up all nuts and fruits from orchards, because all orchards are pollinated by kept bees. Presumably they are also strictly limiting their consumption of coffee and chocolate to "fair traded" brands, since actual human beings are commonly exploited and even enslaved in these industries.

• Maple syrup: This is sap — it's basically tree blood. If you are worried about the pain that inserting the taps causes the trees, you should not buy this product.

• Molasses: This is a product of sugar cane juice and the refining process. The distinctive flavor can overpower milder flavors such as vanilla. Get the unsulfured kind.

NATURAL PRODUCT SOURCES

This list is by no means meant to imply that these are the best companies or products. These are the brands that I most often use because they are readily available at the natural-food store near my house! I'm providing this list simply as a convenience to those readers who are new to the world of natural foods.

Type of Natural Product	See Company(s) #:
apple cider vinegar	5
baking cups, unbleached	2
baking parchment, unbleached	2
baking powder, non-aluminum	21
baking soda	4
birch sugar	27
brown rice syrup	13
canola oil	19, 25
canola oil spray	25
carob powder	6
chocolate chips, dairy-free	20, 26
cocoa powder, fair trade	20
coconut, flaked or shredded	7
coffee substitute, grain-based	17
cream of tartar	11
cream substitute, soy-based	19
egg replacer powder	8
flavored extracts	9, 11
flaked grains	1
flours, whole grain, unbleached	1
lemon juice, organic	22

lime juice, organic 22

molasses, unsulfured 18

nut butters 14

pumpkin, canned, organic 23

sour cream, vegan 24

soymilk 28, 30

soymilk powder 8

soy yogurt 29

spices, organic 11

sugar, dark brown molasses 3

sugar, light brown muscovado 3

sugar, powdered (confectioners') .. 12, 20

sugar, unrefined 10, 20, 29

tofu, silken style 15

waxed paper, unbleached 16

COMPANY CONTACT INFORMATION

1 **Arrowhead Mills, Inc.**
   Box 2059, Hereford, TX 79045 · 800-434-4246
2 **Beyond Gourmet**
   Importer: A. V. Olsson Trading Co., Inc.
   Stamford, CT 06902
3 **The Billington Food Group Ltd.**
   Distributor: Imperial Sugar Company · Sugar Land, TX 77478
4 **Bob's Red Mill National Foods, Inc.**
   5209 S.E. International Way · Milwakie, OR 97222
   www.bobsredmill.com
5 **Bragg**
   Distributor: Live Food Products
   Box 7 · Santa Barbara, CA 93102 · 800-446-1990 · www.bragg.com

6 **Chatfield's**
Distributor: American Natural Snacks · St. Augustine, FL 32084

7 **Edward & Sons Trading Co., Inc.**
Box 1326 · Carpinteria, CA 93014 · www.edwardandsons.com

8 **Ener-G Foods, Inc.**
P.O. Box 84487 · Seattle, WA 98124-5787
800-331-5222 · www.ener-g.com

9 **Flavorganics**
268 Doremus Ave. · Newark, NJ 07105 · 973-344-8014

10 **Florida Crystals Food Corp.**
Palm Beach, FL 33480 · www.FloridaCrystals.com

11 **Frontier Co-Op**
Box 299 · Norway, IA 52318 · www.frontiercoop.com

12 **Hain Pure Foods**
Uniondale, NY 11553 · 800-434-4246 · www.hainpurefoods.com

13 **Lundberg Family Farms**
Richvale, CA · www.lundberg.com

14 **Maranatha Natural Foods**
P.O. Box 1046 · Ashland, OR 97520

15 **Morinaga Nutritional Foods**
P.O. Box 7969 · Torrance, CA 90504
800-669-8638 · www.morinu.com

16 **Natural Value**
Sacramento, CA 95831 · NaturalVal@aol.com

17 **Naturalis Inka**
Importer: Adamba Imports Inc. · Brooklyn, NY 11237

18 **Plantation Barbados Molasses**
Allied Old English, Inc. · Port Reading, NJ 07064

19 **Provamel**
Importer: Pangea Vegan Products
2381 Lewis Avenue · Rockville, MD 20851
301-816-9300 · www.veganstore.com

20 **Rapunzel Pure Organics**
Distributor: efoodpantry
P.O. Box 3483 · Springfield, IL 62708-3483
866-372-6879 · www.rapunzel.com · www.efoodpantry.com

21 **Rumford Baking Powder**
Clabber Girl · Terre Haute · IN 47808 · www.clabbergirl.com

22 **Santa Cruz Organic**
Santa Cruz Natural, Inc.
P.O. Box 369 · Chico, CA 95927 · 530-899-5000

23 **Shari Ann's Organics, Inc.**
P.O. Box 534 · Dexter, MI 48130 · www.shariannsorganic.com

24 **Soymage/Soyco Foods**
Galaxy Nutritional Foods
2441 Viscount Row · Orlando, FL 32809 · www.soyco.com

25 **Spectrum Naturals, Inc.**
133 Copeland Street · Petaluma, CA 94952
spectrumnaturals@netdex.com

26 **Sunspire**
510-686-0116 · San Leandro, CA 94577 · nSpired® Natural Foods

27 **The Ultimate Life**
Box 4308 · Santa Barbara, CA 93140

800-843-6325 · www.ultimatelife.com

28 **Vitasoy USA Inc.**
South San Francisco, CA 94080
800-VITASOY · www.vitasoy-usa.com

29 **Wholesome Sweeteners**
P.O. Box 339 · Savannah, GA 31402

30 **Wholesoy Co.**
San Francisco, CA 94105 · www.wholesoycom.com

INDEX,
BY KEY FLAVORS OR INGREDIENTS

(Some recipes may be listed more than once.)

Flavor or Ingredient	wheat free	nut free /optional	2 tbsp or less oil	no cane sugar	page #
Chocolate					
Banana Muffins		*	*	*	18
Chocolate Scones		*	*		98
Double Chocolate Muffins		*	*		28
Mocha Fudge Coffee Cake	*	*	*		70
Citrus					
Blueberry-Lemon Ring		*	*		54
Lemon Sauce	*	*	*		85
Lemon Scones		*	*		104
Marmalade Muffins		*	*	*	40
Fruit, dried, miscellaneous					
Applesauce Ring		*			50
Applesauce Spice Muffins		*	*		14
Apricot Muffins		*	*	*	16
Carrot Cake Muffins		*	*		22
Cranapple Muffins		*	*	*	26
Date Coffee Cake		*	*		62
Double Rice Muffins	*	*		*	30
Fruit-Full Pear-Date Ring		*		*	64
Hawaiian Fantasy Muffins		*	*	*	38
Oat Bran Muffins		*	*		42
Old-Fashioned Scones		*	*	*	108
Raisin Maple Loaf		*	*	*	76

Flavor or Ingredient	wheat free	nut free /optional	2 tbsp or less oil	no cane sugar	page #
Fruit, fresh, miscellaneous					
Banana Bread		*			52
Banana Muffins		*	*	*	18
Banana Stovetop Scones		*	*	*	92
Blueberry-Lemon Ring		*	*		54
Blueberry-Spelt Muffins		*			20
Breakfast Apple Cake		*	*		56
Fresh Apple or Pear Muffins		*	*	*	34
Fruit-Full Pear-Date Ring		*		*	64
Hawaiian Fantasy Muffins		*	*	*	38
Fruit preserves, miscellaneous					
Applesauce Ring		*			50
Applesauce Spice Muffins		*	*		14
Fruit Preserves Coffee Cake		*	*		66
Marmalade Muffins		*	*	*	40
Mocha Fudge Coffee Cake	*	*			70
Surprise Scones		*	*		114
Grains, miscellaneous					
Blueberry-Spelt Muffins		*			20
Carrot Cake Muffins		*	*		22
Cornmeal Muffins		*	*		24
Cornbread		*			100
Cranapple Muffins		*	*	*	26
Double Rice Muffins	*	*		*	30
Four-Grain Muffins		*			32
Herbed Spelt Squares		*		*	102
Oat Bran Muffins		*	*		42
Oat Scones		*			106
Oatmeal Breakfast Cake		*	*		72

Flavor or Ingredient	wheat free	nut free /optional	2 tbsp or less oil	no cane sugar	page #
Potato-Rice Biscuits	*	*	*	*	110
Spice, miscellaneous					
Applesauce Spice Muffins		*	*		14
Banana Bread		*			52
Carrot Cake Muffins		*	*		22
Carrot Coffee Cake		*	*		58
Crumb-Topped Coffee Cake		*			60
Gingerbread		*	*		68
Gingerbread Lovers' Muffins		*	*		36
Oat Bran Muffins		*	*		42
Oatmeal Breakfast Cake		*	*		72
Old-Fashioned Scones		*	*	*	108
Pumpkin Spice Bread		*			74
Raisin Maple Loaf		*	*	*	76
Very Easy Tea Cake		*			78
Zucchini Bread		*	*		80
Sweeteners, miscellaneous					
Carrot Coffee Cake		*	*		58
Crumb-Topped Coffee Cake		*			60
Crunchy Nutty Topping		*	*		83
Gingerbread		*	*		68
Gingerbread Lover's Muffins		*	*		36
Raisin Maple Loaf		*	*	*	76
Sugar Glaze	*	*	*		87
Vegetables, miscellaneous					
Carrot Cake Muffins		*	*		22
Carrot Coffee Cake		*	*		58
Potato-Rice Biscuits	*	*	*	*	110
Pumpkin Spice Bread		*			74

Flavor or Ingredient	wheat free	nut free /optional	2 tbsp or less oil	no cane sugar	page #
Tomato Biscuits		*		*	116
Zucchini Bread		*	*		80
Other					
Buttermilk-Style Biscuits		*		*	94
Celtic Soda Bread		*	*	*	96
Creamy Topping	*	*	*		82
Frozen Whipped Topping	*	*	*		84
Simple Flavored Muffins		*			44
Stovetop Scones		*		*	112
Vanilla Sauce	*	*	*		86
Very Easy Tea Cake		*			78